KNOW THE NAME; KNOW THE SPIRIT

Discover Your Contract with God in Your Name

Sharón Lynn Wyeth

LightKeepers

Iowa City, Iowa * San Diego, California * Redlands, California * Arcadia, California * Neubrücke, Germany * San Antonio, Texas * Tokyo, Japan * Lincoln, Nebraska * Roswell, New Mexico * Beaverton, Oregon * Longview, Washington * Shanghai, China * Crockett, Texas * Leon Valley, Texas * Hailey, Idaho

First Edition Printing November 2015

Copyright 1st edition © 2015 by Sharón Lynn Wyeth
Copyright issued under the seal of the Copyright Office

Neimology® is a registered trademark, registration #4,008,524
Neimology® Science is a registered trademark exclusively used by the author and others that have been certified by the author to use the trade name.

Publishers contact information available at www.KnowTheName.com

World rights reserved. No part of this publication may be stored in a retrieval system, transmitted, or reproduced in any way, including but not limited to photocopy, photograph, magnetic or other record, without the prior agreement and written permission of the author except in brief quotes used in connection with reviews written specifically for inclusion in a magazine, newspaper or blog.

This book is reference work based upon research by the author. The book contains opinions and ideas of the author. Author intends to offer information of a general nature. Any reliance on the information herein is at the reader's own discretion. The author and publisher specifically disclaim all responsibility for any liability, loss or right, personal or otherwise, which is incurred as a consequence, directly or indirectly, of the use or application of any contents of this book. They further make no representations or warranties with respect to the accuracy or completeness of the contents of this work and specifically disclaim all warranties with respect to the accuracy or completeness of the contents of the work and specifically disclaim all warranties including without limitation any implied warranty of fitness for a particular purpose. Any recommendations are made without any guarantee on the part of the author or publisher. The information as stated in this book is in no way to be considered as a substitute for consultation with a duly licensed psychologist.

Disclaimer: Publishers makes no warranty or representation, either expressed or implied, with respect of the book or of its contents, quality, performance, merchantability, or fitness for a particular purpose. In no event will LightKeepers or its distributors, or dealers be liable to you or any other party for direct, indirect, special, incidental, consequential or other damages arising out of the use of, or inability to use Neimology® Science, even if advised of the possibility of such damage.

Neither the author nor the publisher assumes any responsibility for the use or misuse of information contained in this book.

ISBN #978-1-5193-4141-9
www.KnowTheName.com
Printed in the United States of America

DEDICATION

This book is dedicated to those of us who are on a spiritual path and wish to understand what is expected of us during this particular sojourn on earth. Neimology® Science is the study of the placement of the letters in a name, which then enables us to better understand self at a deeper level simply by interpreting our name. This knowledge is immediately available, as our names are related to how we think, feel and behave as well as our soul's purpose according to our contract with God. Neimology® Science is most useful in helping individuals interpret the clues hidden in their names so that we may know ourselves at a deeper level.

It is also helpful for intrinsically supporting and validating who we currently are. In turn, this saves time and energy in the complicated task of getting to understand why we are here. Neimology® Science assists us in acquiring a new set of skills in comprehending how we function in this world. Essentially, each name holds a key to a person's talents and gifts, and at the same time, identifies one's challenges to be faced in this lifetime. Welcome to a new path of understanding and discovery!

Each individual is born into this life with both talents and challenges. Talents help the person learn and grow which can provide gifts for the rest of the world. Challenges provide a testing ground in order for the person to become strong and resilient and have more compassion for others. Every person born has something to contribute to our world, called gifts, and each has multiple challenges to overcome. Therefore, it is my desire that we not use Neimology® Science as a tool to judge where we are, but rather to assist us along our path so that we can appreciate who we are and in turn appreciate others more fully. It is my sincere desire that this book brings you some answers to the question that we frequently ask self, namely, why am I here?

ACKNOWLEDGEMENTS

Without the help of the following people, this book would not have happened: Colorado Springs, Colorado's Meg Chojnacki (editor and grammar queen), Portland, Oregon's Ann Paes (checked grammar, sentence structures), San Diego, California's Don Cole (photographer and back cover layout), Bar Harbor, Maine's Susan Klopfstein (book cover conception and design), Cypress, California's Dennis Nozawa (book cover artist), Boise, Idaho's Joseph John Dewey (introduction), San Antonio, Texas' Jovanna Robinson Delahay (formatting) and Boise, Idaho's Linda Fujioka (who lovingly took on the task of minimizing my interruptions, so I could actually finish this book). I am grateful for the support of each of these wonderfully talented people. Each has my immense gratitude.

TABLE OF CONTENTS

FOREWORD..xix
INTRODUCTION..xxii
ORIGIN OF NEIMOLOGY® SCIENCE..............................xxv

CHAPTER 1: NAMES 1

CHAPTER 2: FIRST VOWEL IN FIRST NAME ... 20
FIRST VOWEL IS 'A'..30
FIRST VOWEL IS 'E'..34
FIRST VOWEL IS 'I'...40
FIRST VOWEL IS 'O'...44
FIRST VOWEL IS 'U'...49
FIRST VOWEL IS 'Y'..52
ALL VOWELS PRESENT IN A NAME...........................57

CHAPTER 3: FIRST LETTER IN FIRST NAME...59
FIRST LETTER IS 'A'...64
FIRST LETTER IS 'B'...65
FIRST LETTER IS 'C'...66
FIRST LETTER IS 'D'...68
FIRST LETTER IS 'E'...70
FIRST LETTER IS 'F'..71
FIRST LETTER IS 'G'...73
FIRST LETTER IS 'H'...75
FIRST LETTER IS 'I'...77
FIRST LETTER IS 'J'..78
FIRST LETTER IS 'K'...81
FIRST LETTER IS 'L'...83
FIRST LETTER IS 'M'..85
FIRST LETTER IS 'N'...87
FIRST LETTER IS 'O'...89

FIRST LETTER IS 'P' 90
FIRST LETTER IS 'Q' 92
FIRST LETTER IS 'R' 94
FIRST LETTER IS 'S' 96
FIRST LETTER IS 'T' 98
FIRST LETTER IS 'U' 99
FIRST LETTER IS 'V' 101
FIRST LETTER IS 'W' 103
FIRST LETTER IS 'X' 104
FIRST LETTER IS 'Y' 106
FIRST LETTER IS 'Z' 108

CHAPTER 4: LAST LETTER IN FIRST NAME ... 110
LAST LETTER IS 'A' 110
LAST LETTERS ARE 'AH' 111
LAST LETTER IS 'B' 113
LAST LETTER IS 'C' 114
LAST LETTERS ARE 'CK' 116
LAST LETTER IS 'D' 117
LAST LETTER IS 'E' 117
LAST LETTERS ARE 'EY' 119
LAST LETTER IS 'F' 119
LAST LETTER IS 'G' 121
LAST LETTER IS 'H' 124
LAST LETTER IS 'I' 124
LAST LETTER IS 'J' 125
LAST LETTER IS 'K' 126
LAST LETTER IS 'L' 127
LAST LETTER IS 'N' 127
LAST LETTERS ARE 'NN' 128
LAST LETTER IS 'O' 129
LAST LETTER IS 'P' 130
LAST LETTER IS 'Q' 130

LAST LETTER IS 'R' 131
LAST LETTERS ARE 'RK' 132
LAST LETTER IS 'S' 132
LAST LETTER IS 'T' 133
LAST LETTER IS 'U' 134
LAST LETTERS ARE 'UA' 135
LAST LETTER IS 'V' 136
LAST LETTER IS 'W' 136
LAST LETTER IS 'X' 137
LAST LETTER IS 'Y' 138
LAST LETTER IS 'Z' 138

CHAPTER 5: MIDDLE LETTER IN FIRST NAME.. 140
MIDDLE LETTER IS 'A' 143
MIDDLE LETTER IS 'B' 145
MIDDLE LETTER IS 'C' 146
MIDDLE LETTER IS 'D' 148
MIDDLE LETTER IS 'E' 149
MIDDLE LETTER IS 'F' 151
MIDDLE LETTER IS 'G' 152
MIDDLE LETTER IS 'H' 153
MIDDLE LETTER IS 'I' 155
MIDDLE LETTER IS 'J' 156
MIDDLE LETTER IS 'K' 158
MIDDLE LETTER IS 'L' 160
MIDDLE LETTER IS 'M' 163
MIDDLE LETTER IS 'N' 165
MIDDLE LETTER IS 'O' 167
MIDDLE LETTER IS 'P' 168
MIDDLE LETTER IS 'Q' 169
MIDDLE LETTER IS 'R' 169
MIDDLE LETTER IS 'S' 171
MIDDLE LETTER IS 'T' 172

MIDDLE LETTER IS 'U' OR 'V' 174
MIDDLE LETTER IS 'W' 176
MIDDLE LETTER IS 'X' 177
MIDDLE LETTER IS 'Y' 179
MIDDLE LETTER IS 'Z' 179

CHAPTER 6: CONSONANT COMBINATIONS... 181
THE LETTERS 'BR' 183
THE LETTERS 'CH' 184
THE LETTERS 'CHR' 185
THE LETTERS 'CL' 186
THE LETTERS 'CR' 187
THE LETTERS 'DD' 188
THE LETTERS 'DR' 188
THE LETTERS 'FF' 189
THE LETTERS 'FR' 190
THE LETTERS 'GG' 190
THE LETTERS 'GH' 191
THE LETTERS 'GL' 192
THE LETTERS 'GR' 193
THE LETTERS 'HL' 193
THE LETTERS 'HLS' 194
THE LETTERS 'HM' 194
THE LETTERS 'HN' 195
THE LETTERS 'KR' 196
THE LETTERS 'LB' 197
THE LETTERS 'LD' 197
THE LETTERS 'LK' 198
THE LETTERS 'LL' 199
THE LETTERS 'LM' 200
THE LETTERS 'LS' 200
THE LETTERS 'LT' 201
THE LETTERS 'LV' 202

THE LETTERS 'LL'	203
THE LETTERS 'LW'	204
THE LETTERS 'MM'	204
THE LETTERS 'NN'	205
THE LETTERS 'NC'	206
THE LETTERS 'NCH'	206
THE LETTERS 'ND'	207
THE LETTERS 'NR'	208
THE LETTERS 'PH'	208
THE LETTERS 'PR'	209
THE LETTERS 'RB'	210
THE LETTERS 'RC'	210
THE LETTERS 'RD'	211
THE LETTERS 'RH'	212
THE LETTERS 'RG'	213
THE LETTERS 'RK'	214
THE LETTERS 'RL'	214
THE LETTERS 'RM'	215
THE LETTERS 'RR'	215
THE LETTERS 'RT'	216
THE LETTERS 'RTM'	217
THE LETTERS 'SC'	218
THE LETTERS 'SCH'	218
THE LETTERS 'SH'	219
THE LETTERS 'SR'	220
THE LETTERS 'SS'	221
THE LETTERS 'ST'	222
THE LETTERS 'STR'	223
THE LETTERS 'TH'	223
THE LETTERS 'NTH'	224
THE LETTERS 'TR'	225
THE LETTERS 'TT'	225
THE LETTERS 'TTH'	226
THE LETTERS 'TN'	227

THE LETTERS 'TX' AND 'TZ' 227
THE LETTERS 'WH' 228
SUMMARY 230

CHAPTER 7: VOWEL DIPHTHONGS 231
THE 'A' DIPHTHONGS 232
  THE LETTERS 'AA' 232
  THE LETTERS 'AE' 232
  THE LETTERS 'AI' 233
  THE LETTERS 'AO' 233
  THE LETTERS 'AU' 234
  THE LETTERS 'AY' 234
THE 'E' DIPHTHONGS 235
  THE LETTERS 'EA' 235
  THE LETTERS 'EAU' 235
  THE LETTERS 'EE' 235
  THE LETTERS 'EI' 236
  THE LETTERS 'EO' 236
  THE LETTERS 'EU' 237
  THE LETTERS 'EY' 238
THE 'I' DIPHTHONGS 239
  THE LETTERS 'IA' 239
  THE LETTERS 'IE' 239
  THE LETTERS 'II' 239
  THE LETTERS 'IO' 240
  THE LETTERS 'IU' 240
THE 'O' DIPHTHONGS 241
  THE LETTERS 'OU' 241
  THE LETTERS 'OUI' 241
  THE LETTERS 'OUIE' 241
  THE LETTERS 'OY' 242
THE 'U' DIPHTHONGS 242
  THE LETTERS 'UA' 242

THE LETTERS 'UE'	242
THE LETTERS 'UI'	243
THE 'Y' DIPHTHONGS	243
THE LETTERS 'YA'	243
THE LETTERS 'YO'	243
THE LETTERS 'YU'	244

CHAPTER 8: MIXED SYNTACTIC SOUNDS..245

CONSONANTS WITH 'A'	246
THE LETTERS 'AD'	246
THE LETTERS 'AL'	246
THE LETTERS 'AN'	247
THE LETTERS 'AND'	248
THE LETTERS 'ANN'	248
THE LETTERS 'AR'	248
THE LETTERS 'ARA'	249
THE LETTERS 'ARK'	249
THE LETTERS 'ART'	250
THE LETTERS 'ATTI'	250
THE LETTERS 'DAN'	250
THE LETTERS 'GA'	251
THE LETTERS 'HA'	252
THE LETTERS 'MAC'	252
THE LETTERS 'MAL'	252
THE LETTERS 'MAN'	253
THE LETTERS 'NAN'	253
THE LETTERS 'RA'	254
THE LETTERS 'RAY'	254
CONSONANTS WITH THE 'E'	255
THE LETTERS 'ECE'	255
THE LETTERS 'EDE'	256
THE LETTERS 'EL'	256
THE LETTERS 'ELE'	257

THE LETTERS 'EN' 257
THE LETTERS 'ENCE' 257
THE LETTERS 'ENE' 258
THE LETTERS 'ENR' 258
THE LETTERS 'ER' 258
THE LETTERS 'ERE' 259
THE LETTERS 'ESS' 260
THE LETTERS 'EVE' 260
THE LETTERS 'EXE' 261
CONSONANTS WITH THE 'I' 261
THE LETTERS 'CIN' 261
THE LETTERS 'HIM' 262
THE LETTERS 'ICE' 262
THE LETTERS 'IN' 262
THE LETTERS 'LI' 263
THE LETTERS 'SKI' 263
THE LETTERS 'TRI' 264
CONSONANTS WITH THE 'O' 264
THE LETTERS 'GOR' 264
THE LETTERS 'JO' 264
THE LETTERS 'OB' 265
THE LETTERS 'ON' 265
THE LETTERS 'OR' 266
THE LETTERS 'ORG' 267
THE LETTERS 'RO' 267
CONSONANTS WITH THE 'U' 268
THE LETTERS 'BRU' 268
THE LETTERS 'JU' 268
THE LETTERS 'LUC' 269
THE LETTERS 'RU' 269
THE LETTERS 'QU' 270
THE LETTERS 'SUS' 270
THE LETTERS 'UP' 270
THE LETTERS 'UR' 271

    CONSONANTS WITH THE 'Y' 272
    THE LETTERS 'CY' 272
    THE LETTERS 'LY' 272
    THE LETTERS 'LYN' 272
    THE LETTERS 'YN' 273
    THE LETTERS 'YT' 273
    THE LETTERS 'YV' 274

CHAPTER 9: MIDDLE AND LAST NAMES....275

What others are saying about the prequel to
"Know the Name; Know the Spirit"

Received "Award for Literary Excellence" from Books and Authors.net Books of the Year 2007, Books on Names category for Know the Name; Know the Person.

"In my line of work I am given literally hundreds of books every year. I rarely have time to read any of them. But Sharón's book captured my attention. I read it cover to cover and found it to be insightful, enlightening and surprisingly accurate. And it has ended up becoming a very useful and influential tool in both my business and personal life."
Alex Carroll (bestselling author and radio personality)

"This book posits the science of "Neimology®, the study of names" and is groundbreaking, of potentially historic importance, and it affords broad-spectrum practical application. The empirical research and experience behind it has substantial credibility." Amazon review

"I had never heard of such a thing until the author went around the room uncovering personality types based just on their name. It was amazing. I wouldn't have believed it if I hadn't been there to listen how accurately she spelled it out. I find myself "testing" this theory. I think it's amazing." Susi Wong, CEO Good JuJu, Interior Redesign/Home Staging

"Reading this book was an amazing discovery. A door opening to a knowledge that can change the way you live, the way you understand people, the way you interact with people." Linda Malhoyt, store owner

Foreword

By Joseph John Dewey
Author of "THE IMMORTAL" series

Sharón has been a regular speaker at my symposiums and she never fails to entertain and educate the audience. Of all the subjects she has covered none has drawn more interest than her presentation on the meaning of names. Everyone wanted her to interpret their name after she analyzed the meaning of a few names of audience members, and they witnessed how profound her knowledge of the subject was.

As she went through the lucky ones who got analyzed, each seemed not only impressed at her accuracy, but also encouraged by the potential for their own progress that was revealed in their name.

Sharón also told us the interesting story of how she became interested in names. From her youth she felt that there was something wrong with her given name of Sharon. There was something about it that just didn't feel right. She just did not feel like a Sharon. This feeling was not derived from knowledge of names, but from something deep inside of her that she just couldn't shake.

Then, one day her mother introduced her to a slightly different way to pronounce her name; Sharón, (pronounced Shah-rone) instead of Sharon. This new pronunciation struck a chord with her and just felt right. She immediately changed her name and her life, which seemed to be a little out of balance. The new enunciation just seemed to be much more in tune with her life's purpose. This event also renewed her interest in names and sent her on a quest and that was to discover all of the hidden meanings in our names.

Yes, I know, standard numerology has been around for a long time and reveals a few things about the meaning of numbers in relation to words and names. However, Sharón had not been exposed to numerology, instead she started from scratch doing her own research into the patterns found in names. Sharón goes far beyond any other book on name interpretation that I have seen.

She has discovered many nuances that reveal meanings where we never realized there was meaning, and purpose where we never realized there was purpose. For instance, she teaches about the meaning of each letter of the alphabet and notes additional meanings in various combinations. She explains that there is a difference in the meaning of vowels and consonants. The first letter of your name has special meaning as well as how the various sounds resonate.

When Sharón first told me she was writing a book on interpreting names I thought she was working on a standard explanation of numerology, but was I ever wrong on that assumption.

Her two books on names break new ground and will set a new standard on name interpretation, which I believe will stand the test of time and become a new foundation for knowledge on the subject that others will use for generations to come.

JJ Dewey, as he is known, is the prolific author of <u>The Immortal</u> Series and other works. He leads an online class for the group "Keysters" that discusses, in depth, interpretations of the Bible.

INTRODUCTION

Before coming to earth we know our purpose. We know why we are choosing to have an earthly experience and why we have chosen this time in which to participate on the earth. We also get to preview our roughest times, which accounts for déjà vu moments, and any contracts that we have in place that involve another. For instance, we may have a contract to get married or to buy a particular house at a particular time. Thus we will be pulled to go in a certain direction in order to fulfill our contracts with others. Then we are born into a physical body.

In many ways our culture determines our openness to Spirit. One is more likely to be open to the idea that what happens in this lifetime may have had its origin in another lifetime when born into a culture that accepts the ideas of reincarnation and karma. Born into a culture that refutes the ideas of reincarnation and karma leaves a person wondering what they did that caused such incidents to occur in this lifetime. This often causes the person to blame others for what occurs, negating their own involvement in creating their current situations.

Regardless of the cultural influences, the soul seeks experiences to learn and grow. The soul seeks knowledge and a mind-heart connection to advance itself along its path. Thus, the soul will pull and push the personality in order to urge it into cooperation. Occasionally the personality will choose one way while the soul chooses another. Thus the first book in this series is, Know the Name; Know the Person which delves into how our personality works and the desires and traits of the personality. This book, Know the Name; Know the Spirit is its companion which expresses the soul's desires for growth. It gives insights into what your soul came to learn in order for you to grow in your awareness with the end goal of creating a higher consciousness.

An interesting side note to Neimology® Science is the science of Acrophonology, which states that names influence both a person's character and life path. Unfortunately, Acrophonology does not tell anyone how to determine what that influence will be without looking it up in a book. This is no different from books that give a short interpretation of each name as none informs those interested how to ascertain the influence of a name for oneself, which is the goal of this book. Neimology® Science is another way of saying the science of the Light of the Soul.

In order to raise our vibration, our understandings, our level of consciousness, we all must eventually align our personality with our soul's desires as our soul's aim is to help us reunite with our Creator by remembering and honoring that spark of divinity, the light, that lives within us all. Each letter resonates to its own vibration. Thus, each name is a symphony composed of the vibrations of the individual letters coupled with playing some letters at the same time which creates new vibrations.

To that aim, Spirit has brought forth these two books, (Know the Name; Know the Person and Know the Name; Know the Spirit) to assist you in reuniting these two parts, personality and soul, in your endeavor to fully remember Love and Light in all of It's glory. May you find these books a useful tool, and may our Creator continue to bless you along your path.

ORIGIN OF NEIMOLOGY® SCIENCE

Whatever one does repeatedly, one will eventually find a shortcut to do the same thing more efficiently. In my case, it was a combination of excelling at seeing patterns and sequences, which derived from life experiences, formal education, and teaching math. It started with my studies in junior high, expanded while a mathematics major in college and continued with frequent moves as an adult where I learned how to quickly discern what the rules/procedures were at each new location. This created an ability to effectively observe others, which was further developed by interacting with literally thousands of people as a teacher and later as a school administrator. Finally, this power to identify useful patterns has been greatly refined by my ongoing work with others on their spiritual journeys.

When I was creating seating charts at the beginning of my seventh year of teaching, certain patterns began to emerge in names. I automatically wanted males whose names started with the letter 'J' to sit where they would not distract other children and where I could supervise them closely. I did not want children with the first vowel of 'U' to sit too closely to other children who also had the first vowel of 'U' as I didn't want them to entertain each other with their playfulness. Creating seating charts to maximize an effective, disciplined classroom was how I started to discover the patterns that later developed into Neimology® Science.

Realizing that some part of me had received impressions, I questioned what other patterns I could find. It was easiest to find similarities in whole first names like what every David or Julie had in common versus what the individual letters stated. However, over a period of twenty-two years in education and interacting with a multitude of people, I was able to single out the individual letters and combinations of letters that were associated with different patterns.

The greatest boon to this investigation, led by my curiosity, was when I was hired as Vice-Principal and had the opportunity to discipline high school children. Previously, as an administrator, I had always held roles where I was the creative problem solver and hence the 'good' guy; thus, this was a rare opportunity. I was kept so busy that I didn't fully realize how valuable a gift it had been until after I left that job.

Before this experience, I was only able to discern the gifts or positive attributes of the letters within each name. In contrast, this new role allowed me to work with many children who wanted to skirt the rules, plus their parents, many of whom did not want to see their children have to take responsibility for their own choices. This provided me with a lot of experiential data that I could use to continue the search for patterns in both the children's and adults' behaviors and approaches to life in general. Hence I was able to piece together many of the common challenges faced by those with certain letters, and letter clusters, in their names.

When I left the education field, I temporarily put aside my explorations of names and started using my skills to assist people to grow spiritually. After assisting hundreds of clients, I realized that Neimology® Science was also beneficial in this endeavor. My interest was truly reinvigorated.

After fifteen years of combining my intellect, observational skills, experiences and spiritual work, and another year of testing my observations, I put together a workshop in which to share the information. I trusted that if people found fault in my reasoning, they would challenge me and I would be able to fine-tune the system. I also wanted to see if Neimology® Science was equally effective in countries that spoke languages other than English, but used the same alphabetic symbols. During my travels and teaching sessions over the next three years in parts of Europe, Africa, North, Central and South America, Asia, India, and Israel, I found that with only a few adjustments for transliterated names, the system of gaining knowledge about people by analyzing their names worked in these countries as well.

There are many books printed on what a name means, from the Druid interpretation to the Hebrew interpretations. However, to my knowledge, this is the first book that breaks down the name to show where the interpretation originates. This is reclaiming the old science of nomenology in a modern way.

It is with pleasure that I present to you Neimology® Science or the study of the placement of letters in a name. This may start you on your own path of observation. I encourage you to test the usefulness and accuracy of this information for yourself and to add your own insights and inspirations.

CHAPTER 1: NAMES

"One day you will know your divine purpose. It is written in your name." Joseph John Dewey

We can fight, we can scream, we can swear, we can be a willing participant, we can do anything we like; however, nothing we do will change what it is that the soul wishes to accomplish in this lifetime. We cannot go easily against our destiny as higher forces control such things. When we attempt to go against our destiny, we usually live miserable lives as we have gone against the very reasons why we are here and rebelled against learning our lessons. Each of us has our own purpose, distinct and different from everyone else. Our Creator has shown us that uniqueness is what is valued; each of us being a bit different from everyone else. Even our fingerprints exemplify this idea just as each snowflake is different from every other snowflake.

Spirit, soul, and life's purpose are things that we hear plenty about but take our entire lives to figure out as we are born in forgetfulness of who we are and why we are here. Thus, life circumstances have been created prior to our births to help remind us of the divine plan for us. When we become more conscious of our mission, it helps both us and those around us, as it helps to heal others that share our presence due to our ability to understand others' experiences.

At one time there were seven major religions upon the earth, and they all agreed on the basic tenets but disagreed on how to present those tenets. They cooperated with each other to educate and share sacred knowledge when someone was interested.[1] One of the commonly held understandings was that the incoming soul impressed upon the person – one of the parents, the oldest adult male, the local shaman, who

---
1 Nine Faces of Christ by Dr. Eugene Whitworth

would be naming the baby what the soul wanted to be called. So, in essence, it was understood that we name ourselves.

These people, who chose themselves to be dedicated to higher growth, became initiates. It did not matter which of the seven pathways[2] was chosen as they all led to the same result. This is no different from math and the multiplicity of ways to solve a problem. Suppose one has simultaneous equations to solve. You can solve two equations with two unknowns by graphing the lines, by using substitution, by executing elimination rules or by using a matrix. Each person will find one of these four ways easier than the others; yet all four get the correct answer for you. The same could be said about the seven spiritual pathways.

Some of today's religions have tweaked what was once taught by using parts of the truth, embellishing other parts, or deleting some parts in their records entirely thereby totally omitting important data. This was done out

---

[2] In ancient times the pathways were: Confucianism, Druidism, Hinduism, Judaism, Mittannic-Nordic, Sharramanic, and Zoroastrianism. Today the seven major religions are: Buddhism, Christianity, Confucianism, Hinduism, Islam, Judaism, and Taoism. Notice only Confucianism and Judaism are in both groups.

of the ruse that each person did not have the capability of discerning for himself what ought to be believed. So, others made decisions for us and let us know there was no reason to think for ourselves. Even some of our most sacred books have been mistranslated from their original language: parts left out and other parts changed.[3] For example, why is one version of the Bible called the King James Version? It is called that because King James modified the existing Bible of his day to his liking.[4]

There are so many untruths in our world today. So many lies surround us: from people not being who they truly are; to our newscasters spinning the news; to government officials outright lying to the public assuming we are too ignorant to recognize the lies. Our parents lie to us with good intentions telling us about Santa Claus, the Easter Bunny and the Tooth Fairy. Our history books lie as they reveal the idealized version of what really happened, as the winners of any war are the ones that write the history books. How are we ever to recognize the

---
[3] The Council of Nicaea altered the existing Bible and decided what books should stay and which should not. Additionally they did their best to eliminate all references to reincarnation and karma besides denigrating women. More at http://www.livescience.com/2410-council-nicea-changed-world.html
[4] The Christian Conspiracy by David L. Moore.

truth when it is surrounded by so many lies? It is no wonder that we grow up confused with all of these lies surrounding us. Perhaps that is why "the truth shall set you free" is such a powerful statement.

Most people want the same things: they want a roof over their heads; food in their bellies; and education and happiness for their families. Most people wish to be good. Most of us do the best we can with the knowledge that we currently have. This includes our parents, even as we may have disagreed with them. Most of us want to know the truth. How do we find it, recognize it, and discern which parts are eternal truths? To do this, we must go inside, shed our fears about not knowing, and listen to our hearts and our souls. We shall be led by that spark of Light that we all carry within us.

First we must get to know self and not be afraid of what we find. We must have the courage to acknowledge all parts of self: including the good, the bad and the ugly, and accept who we are in this particular moment. Thus, we give self the freedom of choice to change the parts of us that no longer work, the parts of us that live in fear, and the parts of us that we judge. We can transform these parts by first identifying what they are and how they serve us.

Reasons exist for almost everything. Not much happens by accident. You are here to learn and to grow in your awareness and to be of service to others. You are on a mission to raise your consciousness. By doing so, you shall also assist the people around you to raise theirs. Going against your soul's desires causes suffering. Following your soul's desires creates knowledge that eventually leads to outer joy and unbridled inner joy.

Where the book, Know the Name; Know the Person introduces the entire Neimology® Science system and how it works, this book continues from there and builds on those basic skills looking at the letters from a spiritual perspective versus the personality perspective. Whereas Know the Name; Know the Person is best read starting at page one and continuing page by page, this book is to be used as a reference. You can look up each letter in your name by its position and read what that letter or that letter combination says about your purpose, your mission, and why you are here. In order not to become overwhelmed I suggest that you read one letter at a time and incorporate that learning into your life before continuing to the next letter or letter combination.

Before continuing, we need to address what happens to those people who change their names once they are here. For example, many women change their last name when getting married, people use nicknames, others abbreviate their names using only their initials and still others add superlatives like Mrs. or Dr. to their name. A person's first name is the essence of who they are. The middle name represents the qualities and characteristics that show up under stress; it can also represent one's immediate past life or the culmination of experiences from previous lifetimes that are affecting this lifetime. The last name indicates influences from our environment, and that does change over time. All names are important and contribute to why we are here.

When one changes his first and/or middle name, does his contract with God also change?

Yes, and no. What I have found having done thousands of name readings is the vast majority of times, the person may change his name yet the purpose remains intact. They are attempting to manage their goals from a different perspective, from a different angle. There are multiple ways of accomplishing one's goals, and normally the name change simply alters the way the person goes about his learning, but not what the soul came to experience.

There are those rare occasions when one alters his name, and now the goals have changed. In those cases, I have found that the person normally acquires alternative knowledge with the name change. Then the person's inner guidance system has more work to do to make sure the soul has the opportunities to learn what was indicated in the original name. It is as if our consciousness is our back-up plan. So, please do not worry if you have changed any of your names. All names cause one to continually grow, and all knowledge is valuable. This can also be compared to attending college. Many students start with one goal, or major, and along the way change their minds.

In doing research for this book, it became apparent that we do our greatest harm to ourselves when we live our lives for another or allow someone else to make our decisions for us. As Steve Jobs states, "Your time is limited, so don't waste it living someone else's life. Don't be trapped by dogma – which is living with the results of other people's thinking. Don't let the noise of other's opinions drown out your own inner voice. And most important, have the courage to follow your heart and intuition." When it happens that we live our life by another's' dictates, we temporarily forget who we are. Then our contract with God may not get accomplished. So how do we live our lives such that we know that they are fully lived and fulfill our original contract with God?

According to one of my favorite spiritual practitioners Daskalos, also known as The Magus of Strovolos, as stated in his book, Esoteric Teachings, the entire three-dimensional universe is created and continuously maintained by "Thought Form Elementals" of the great Seraphim Archangels. It is my feeling that names assist Thought Form

Elementals in doing just that as the expression of your full name is the totality of your personal evolution of your experiences, talents, and knowledge over this entire lifetime.

Why are you here? What did you come to do? What is the purpose of your life? These are all questions we have asked ourselves at one time or another. Wouldn't it be wonderful if the answer were easy to find and even easier to know, let alone accomplish? People have tried many alternative methodologies in search of meaning and clues to who we are. These clues exist in our facial features, in our palms, and in our handwriting. Yet we still question. Why are we here?

If we were going to go into a holodeck, like on the television show Star Trek, we would ask the program to deliver the situation and settings that would best suit our purpose for this particular trip to the holodeck. We may choose to go into the holodeck by ourselves, or more frequently, we would choose to play our part with our friends so that we would know that someone had our backs. They would also understand the goal of this particular sojourn for us, just as we would know our friend's goals as they would often overlap. Some of our friends may have other commitments at the time we choose to enter the holodeck so they enter later to join us. Others may have preceded us. Some of us may decide to have alternative beginnings even though we entered the holodeck at approximately the same time so that we meet up after we've each had our different adventures. Regardless of when our friends enter the deck, we will eventually meet them if we have made that agreement prior to entering the holodeck.

We structure the holodeck as to which period of time we would like to experience. Just as time is a construct and exists as a structure that we move through. So we choose our beginning and ending dates. Thus the holodeck's experiences do not have to be linear any more than our lifetimes have to be. For example, we could experience the time period of the signing of our Declaration of Independence. Then the next trip to the holodeck we could experience the time period where Magellan sails around the world or Buddha is sitting under his tree. We are constructing our destiny in the holodeck. It is not designed by another and then forced upon us.

It would be boring if everything in the holodeck went perfectly: the right lighting, beautiful scenery and filled with laughter. We need a challenge to grow. Even in the board games that we play, we give ourselves a challenge, as without one, we soon tire of playing. Thus, when we enter the holodeck we have a light side and a shadow side. Said another way, we give ourselves gifts and challenges as that is what makes the game exciting and worth playing. Each of us has both qualities, a light side and a shadow side, just in varying degrees.

To make our experience that much more fun we interconnect our thought forms with the holodeck so that our thoughts help guide the programming. Thus, when in the holodeck, our belief systems are not based in reality but in our perception of reality.

So, we set the holographic program to our liking. We choose the time frame that we wish to move through and we pick the people who will play with us. Thus, we help create the surroundings that we will experience. Once we enter the holodeck, the game, the realm of possibilities, everything seems so real that it is quite easy to forget our part in setting the stage for what we find. Our focus naturally goes toward what is happening in the holographic deck and we easily forget what happened before our entering the holographic space, just as it does once we're born on Earth. Could earth be considered a holographic creation for our spirit selves?

What happens when we get into the program and don't like our creation? First, we must remember our part in the creation of it so that we can then choose to change the programming. However, not many of us do that, instead blaming others or worse yet, shutting down too soon to stop our feelings in order to protect self since we don't feel adequate for the job. Some of us even pretend ignorance. We must confront our feelings to stay on the path that is right for us.

Needing safety, or submerging our feelings in lieu of managing them, keeps us occupied with unimportant things and takes us off path. We run or consider ourselves pushed off path when we run from our past instead of embracing it and doing our best to understand why things occurred as they did. What were our lessons? What did we take away from the experience? If we do not take time to reflect and consider alternate ways to view our past, we end up being scattered in our emotions. That is the result of our past pushing us instead of us taking charge of who we are now.

We have peace once we truly know ourselves. We are uncomfortable and often avoid what we need to heal. Avoidance comes from judgment which stems from seeing in another what we don't like in ourselves. Avoidance is a result of fear. If you avoid something, you are afraid of it. Do you fear to look at a potential issue when someone brings up an unpleasantry? It is much easier to blame someone or something else versus acknowledging our part in the creation of what happened. Yet you only have the power to change things once you've taken responsibility for them. Acceptance of self is the key[5].

Our faces reflect what has occurred in our

---

[5] www.psychologytoday.com/blog/valley-girl-brain/201307/why-we-are-the-way-we-are

lives. So, let's digress for just a moment and look at the big chicken-or-egg puzzle that runs throughout face perception research. Do the biological blessings behind good looks cause a sparkling personality; or do attractive people exhibit the socially desirable traits of extraversion and agreeableness because society treats swans better than ugly ducklings? Or do individuals with attractive personalities develop more attractive faces over time? Whether nature or nurture, the relationship between beauty and "positive" personality traits is real – and readily discernible[6]. Both nature and nurture affect a person's beauty as the two qualities, or influences, are inseparable. Does the face we're born with reflect the way we behave, which influences how others see us, which then affects the way we behave? This question cuts to the heart of identity. [7]

It is similar with names. Do people with "good" names give rise to a sparkling personality? Do attractive people exhibit the socially desirable traits of extraversion and agreeableness because society treats people with

---
6 http://www.psychologytoday.com/basics/beauty
7 www.psychologytoday.com/basics/identity

common and easy to pronounce names better, or does the name contribute to the personality? Are those people with "bad" names doomed? All names have both gifts and challenges and, to me, there is no "good" or "bad" name. The real question is whether the name has enough appropriate gifts so that the challenges can be overcome. Your name indicates the extent of your gifts and challenges, the ease of each lesson to be learned, and the personality predispositions to how those characteristics shall be exhibited, even as those initial qualities are inherent from the soul. Said simply, some names yield an easier time in life than others.

If I had one of the "worst" names, I'd want to know what made it that way and if there were gifts in the name that could be developed. The only reason a name is in the "worst" category is because those names come with hard challenges per current cultural norms. (Just so you know), the letters 'D', 'J' and 'H' have an overabundance of gifts versus challenges and the inverse is true with the letters 'F', 'G', 'L' and 'Z'. For example, one of the qualities in each of those letters are: 'F's signify a propensity to exaggerate the truth; 'G's signify a temptation to addictions,; 'L's can have serious health challenges that can be misdiagnosed, and 'Z's have a challenging time learning from others.

The benefit of a difficult name is that those individuals also have the opportunity to progress the most and to gain the most from this lifetime. A person does not grow very much when a name doesn't have many challenges. People with easy tasks in their name could be considered to be experiencing a vacation lifetime, or some could consider it as almost like a wasted lifetime. People with easy names have not been challenged, so when really tough emotional situations happen they flounder as they do not know how to handle the difficult situations. However, this is not true for the people with the "worst" names. Given enough time they can cope with anything that comes their way, because their name has made them strong. There is no judgment involved with names. Names are all subject to what the soul wishes to accomplish. The vast majority of names have a near equal amount of gifts and challenges.

Attributes of names were discussed in Know the Name; Know the Person. The first letter of the name is the first impression that is given to others, and the last letter in the first name is the lasting impression others have of you. The vowels represent our emotions, and consonants represent our attitudes.

In comparison, when looking at names from a spiritual perspective, the first letter in your name represents what becomes the most important aspect of this life, and the last letter in your first name is a major tool to be used in achieving that goal. There is always the challenge of living our "life" for someone else and not for "self". When that is the case, we run the risk of forgetting who we are and not fulfilling our contract for this lifetime.

Vowels still represent our feelings; yet, vowels also announce when we are giving our power away to others instead of listening to our inner voice. Vowels help us to see where emotional detachment becomes more logical while not denying our feelings, instead feeling them to the fullest.

Consonants are current beliefs. As David

Eagleman says in his book, Incognito, "You are not perceiving what's out there. You are perceiving whatever your brain tells you." Consonants are constantly asking us to question what beliefs we hold and why. Are our beliefs something we simply accept as that is what we were taught, or are they something that we experienced, and as such, life has shown us that is the way it is? Life shows us Universal Laws versus being taught mankind's laws. Consonants indicate where we may have myopic viewpoints that need to change so that we can become more conscientious.

So how do we live our lives such that we know that they were fully lived, and more importantly, that we have fulfilled our purpose for being here? When we understand our nature, we can consciously align with our destiny.

Things manifest when destiny and free will are in alignment. Neimology® Science interprets your name to reveal a personalized roadmap. We develop a relationship with twenty-six variables, or letters, as we embody this energy in our names. The letters, individually and in combination with other letters, guide us toward profound wisdom.

CHAPTER 2:
FIRST VOWEL IN FIRST NAME

"Our names are not happenstance by any means." Richard Andrew King

Vowels in our names represent our emotions and what emotional lessons we are here to learn. They also indicate whether we learn first from our emotions or from tapping into our soul's desires. Said another way, the vowels indicate how we use our emotions. Do our emotions dominate us, or have we learned to experience emotions without giving into them?

Vowels share with us where our deepest wounds are and where we can lack self-esteem or self-respect. Vowels also announce when we are giving our power away to others instead of listening to our inner voice. Prior to building our confidence in the areas represented by the vowels, we will tend to over compensate and generously give away our power regarding these tendencies in order to feel all right about ourselves. This can lead to subservience and the endless need to prove ourselves in these areas to both self and to others. Due to over compensation, these areas tend to become our strengths, even if we don't recognize them as such.

Vowels help us to see where emotional detachment may be necessary and even where more logic may be of assistance. We are not here to deny our feelings; instead, we are to feel them to the fullest. That does not mean that we must act on each feeling we have, nor express each feeling. As the Thai meditation master Ajahn Chah has stated when referring to the Buddha's teachings: "It is essential to find that right balance, balance that holds onto nothing and yet rejects nothing."[8] That is how we are to address our feelings, hold onto nothing and yet reject nothing. Our feelings and our emotions,

---
[8] "Food for the Heart: The Teachings of Ajahn Chah" by Ajahn Chah

when used properly, are tools that help us grow and are fabulous motivators to help us want to change.

Many humans feel unloved, misunderstood, unexplored, unrecognized and empty. To grow in consciousness one has to unlearn and peel off all such negative emotional feelings for truth has no feelings, no considerations, no interpretations, no commitments, and no blemishes. Truth simply is.

Emotions help us to look at self, to see the perfect human in ourselves, so that we may develop into it. It may be a struggle, but it is possible to conquer the demons of ego's humiliation and self-destructive habits. Consider the idea that Billy Grimsley[9] espouses in his work regarding how to heal grief, "Feelings originate in our thoughts as they relate to our identity." Keeping this simple; when we change our thoughts, our feelings also change.

Per Dr. Allan Botkin,[10] "A person experiences

---

9 Miracles; A Shift in Perception by Billy Grimsley, a specialist in grief therapy.

10 Induced After Death Communication, A New Therapy for Healing Grief and Trauma by Dr. Allan Botkin, PhD with R. Craig Hogan, PhD., who discovered the Induced after-death communication, IADC, technique that heals the deep sadness that is associated with the death of a loved one. http://www.induced-adc.com/

a healing from within." To paraphrase Botkin, it is our ability to understand situations, and other people, that relieves us from grief, anger and guilt and transforms those feelings into contentment.

Per Joseph John Dewey[11], feelings originate in the mind of God. Regardless, feelings are tools that help us slow down, to reassess and to reflect previous decisions. What would we like to keep, and what would we to do or feel differently next time? In other cases, when feeling great, what did we do that we would like to repeat?

Feelings assist us in developing compassion. Compassion is a powerful emotion that one feels in response to the suffering of others which, in turn, motivates a desire for us to help others. It was through compassion that Yeshua[12] Ben Joseph, better known as Jesus, was able to create the space where people could heal.

We grow from being stimulated from outside of us and verifying information from within us.[13] Feelings are what we call our inside

---

11 Joseph John Dewey, author of The Immortal series, at his yearly Conference in Boise, Idaho, June 2014. Transcripts available at www.freeread.com
12 Hebrew name
13 Ibid

verification process. Again, per JJ Dewey, "Feelings originate inside of us. We can choose to share them or not. Emotions mean to emote. Emotions are feelings radiating out from you."[14] To summarize, we receive feelings from the mind of God, and they are what we feel internally. When the feelings are expressed outwardly, they are emotions. Both feelings and emotions are tools that we use to help us grow in our awareness, and both must remain as tools to use and not to overtake us or to become more important than our thoughts.

Our souls are endless, old, and predefined in such a way that many of us, sometime during our lifetime, start to feel starved of Light. It feels as if we are not able to feel continuous joy and the connection to oneness no matter what we do. When the soul is starved of Light, it starts looking for pacifiers, such as, wanting to help others. This is not a bad desire. However, it is often breaking the role of cause and effect.

By being excessively helpful, we might disturb one's natural environment and development of the karmic pattern. This is similar to a net that is woven but with some holes in it. Some may

---
[14] Ibid

consider themselves helpful and sew up the holes. Yet, the holes make it possible for small fish to slip through and not be caught. The small fish were not supposed to be caught in the first place. The net was perfect exactly how it was designed before helpful people interfered.

So, how are we to know when to help and when not? Basically, we help when the person is already on his path and by assisting, we can make it a bit easier or faster. Suppose a single mother is working a job to pay for her schooling, attending college and doing the best she can to spend quality time with her children. We can offer to reimburse her part or all of her tuition for courses she has finished, and has earned a grade of eighty percent or higher. She would have already completed the course, earned her grade, and now, by being reimbursed a portion of her tuition, we are helping her work fewer hours to earn the tuition for her next courses, and thus have more time with her children. She is already on her path; we are simply making it easier for her to succeed.

Take this same scenario for someone who states they wish to go to college, gets tuition paid up front by way of a scholarship, and then is too lazy to do the work and eventually drops out. The money was wasted, the person was not helped, as there was not a willingness to work and thus give value to what was freely given.

There are many people who are being harmed by being helped. Help is totally misunderstood. Help means support to learn. This is a different viewpoint to consider. Help means support to learn and believing in someone when they are having a difficult time believing in self. We have the key, given to us in our names, to be able to see beyond the immediate, and that is what we are supposed to do.

With a vision of the now, we are acting outdated because the now is over before we can act on it. Feelings help to keep us in the now. Let spirit take care of the now. We are encouraged to learn to look beyond. To develop into the light keepers that we are, we must avoid getting off path, which is what we can do when caught up in emotions.

"Feel blessed to do a wrong step; please do not feel upset when you realize that you have gone after the mighty dollar or have been drawn into someone else's drama. It is a blessing to see the blunders. Most people on earth do not recognize their missteps, and when they feel them because of the resulting disasters, they end up blaming others for their choices." [15]

The light worker opens his entire being to the wonderful light that is awaiting him. You will find your path. You will find that wonderful old spirit that is your twin soul guiding you. It is your own soul. Do not search outside. It is where you are. Your life will change most likely so dramatically that you will sit and cry and distribute your tears of happiness. The day will come when you truly find life and love and light.

Remember that feelings of love and light that you hold back from others through fear-based emotions will fade away from you, as they are not shared. Feelings based in fear take you off your spiritual path. So many souls are tired as they are confronted with too many things that are hard to digest. Your soul is sad and will rebel to the extent that you feel separate from yourself. That is when selfishness is kicking in and soul pain will grow like a cancer until it is fleeing the body.

---

15   Trudy Dannhart-Voss, Canadian author's personal e-mail

Please do not do that to yourself or others. Periodically taking time out from the busy world, while staying in silence, is a way to find your spiritual path again. Only then you can find real love, happiness and inner peace.

Each of the vowels in a name holds where our heart yearns to feel emotions, or not to feel emotions by suppressing our feelings. Vowels also indicate where our emotions are either supporting us or keeping us from growing into the Light of the Soul.

Relationships can cause us problems when our expectations of another person are not realized. However, when we understand how the communication style, represented in the first vowel acts, what is going on inside of the other person, it is easier for us not to take things personally, and to see with compassionate eyes what the other person is experiencing.

There may come some times in your life when you choose to walk away from people who create drama for the sake of drama. Hanging in my classroom is a poster that said, "Attention all Drama Queens: Auditions have been cancelled for today."[16] Instead you can choose

---
16 Poster made by artist named Jewels

to surround yourself with people who make you laugh. Let the past be your past. Love the people who treat you right, and pray for them while also including the ones who do not support you. Life is too short to be anything but happy. Falling down is a part of life; getting back up is living.

Remember, desire is magic, and passion is action.

FIRST VOWEL IS 'A'

If you have the first vowel of 'A', then your soul came to learn a lot. You wish to make full use of your time here on earth, and so you stacked the deck on what you wished to accomplish.

When you have the first vowel of 'A', you tend to give and give and give of yourself in order to feel better about you. You often worry unnecessarily about your performance even if you are good enough. Thus you either work extra hard and become a workaholic to prove to yourself your own worth, or you become a laggard as you are too lazy to even begin something as you realize how much work it will be and you do not feel that you have enough knowledge to do it justice. Why bother if you already know you are not going to succeed?

A side effect of not feeling good enough about self is you can become a workaholic attempting to prove your value through your work. It is important to remember that even God rested after creating the world, for the seventh day was a day of rest.

Often you will vacillate between these two positions and can work until you drop from shear exhaustion. You tend to be very hard on yourself and are often more generous with others than with self. Your challenge here is to monitor your self-talk, reaffirming what you consider your positive characteristics versus those that you are judging.

You do not need outside criticism, as you are very good at criticizing self. This is a side effect of not feeling good enough and having to prove your worth to self and to others. Thus, you are here to learn that it is futile to try to prove your self worth, as it never works; instead, to accept you for who you are.

Since you feel devastated when criticized and want to shut down and quit, you compensate by boosting others' confidences, even as you forget to boost your own. Thus, it is important for you to see the good that you do and not to focus on negative actions for otherwise you can get lost in self-judgment. The soul does not wish to judge or be judged, simply accepted. The challenge for your soul is to see itself as equal and once it does, not to stretch this found knowledge into also thinking that you are better than others.

Your tendency is to self-sacrifice for the good of the whole in order to feel appreciated and valued. Unfortunately, many do not see what you have done on their behalf and this reinforces your feeling of unworthiness. So, the soul is encouraged to create a feeling of self-worth from within instead of seeking affirmation from without.

You are highly observant and will take in most of what occurred. However, whatever small part you have missed haunts you and causes you to obsess over the portion that was missed versus reminding yourself of the huge portion that was observed. This causes you to move toward perfectionism, which is deadly as then you can become even more judgmental, especially toward self. So, you have come to learn that it is okay to have self-confidence. It is okay to stand up for self.

It is okay to observe and just be the witness for others without the need to do anything. The goal is to realize that you are good enough just the way you are.

You are not susceptible to guilt or

subservience as easily as other first vowels may be. You balk at taking directions that make no sense. However, since you desire peace above self-satisfaction, you tend to stay quiet to keep the peace more often than not. You are here to learn how to feel comfortable putting your foot down, how to say no amicably, and to assert your truth in order to bring situations back into balance. Your soul wishes for you to learn how to comfortably express your true desire so your aspirations may be fulfilled.

To stay in balance, remember to give yourself the required time to inwardly reflect and inwardly to verify the outward signs that you have received. When you seek quiet time away from others, it is to create a balancing act within yourself, and you are not to be admonished, nor consider yourself rude when insisting that others honor your private time. Time alone is a necessary action for you to be able to stay in balance. Without this balance, you will lean toward the negative view of life, versus the positive. Your soul strongly desires peace and positive experiences so time alone to consider other views is crucial to your soul's progression.

FIRST VOWEL IS 'E'

Learning goes through many stages. The first is to learn mastery over the physical body, and the second is to learn mastery over the emotional body. You have come to learn how to master your emotions so that they don't become the master of you. You often feel an empty, nagging spot within your own heart as you seek emotional fulfillment. You seek to be completed, to feel bliss on earth. You often feel this can only be accomplished through receiving another's love. So, how do you get people to give you genuine love? By becoming the object of your own love first, by loving you. You came to learn how to love yourself so that others may also love you. You did not come to love another in the hopes that the love would be returned to you in the manner and way that you would like it. The love you seek must originate within you and must stay in a pure state. It cannot be a selfish love, which will never be satisfied. Only a pure heart shall allow you to love yourself in the manner that you seek. So you came to experience the purity of honest, selfless love.

As stated in the first book on Neimology® Science, Know the Name; Know the Person, "'E's learn from their feelings and are generally able to express a wide range of emotions, unless they choose the other extreme which is fear of emotion. Emotional fear expresses itself in denial, which then causes a repression of the emotion. People with the first vowel of 'E' are sensitive in the area of feelings and understand the importance of discussing them."

Your soul wishes to express your emotional needs without a feeling of awkwardness when doing so. Thus it is important to have a large vocabulary filled with feeling words in order to express yourself clearly. Words need to be able to go beyond feeling mad, sad, glad and angry. Words need to include depressed, inhibited, embarrassed, disregarded, unappreciated, etc. Since you have come to have the experience of expressing yourself without inhibitions, you may occasionally have a tendency to dramatize the emotions, either internally or externally. Emotional satisfaction may seem just out of reach. When you do share your emotions, you may feel guilty that you did so later, and attempt to revert back to acting as if that dramatization never really happened. Your soul wishes to find the balance in knowing how to express itself using emotions while simultaneously being careful not to suppress the emotions to make others feel better. Your soul will be in conflict with your personality when you are excessively dramatic in an attempt to make yourself feel better or when you suppress your feelings or overeat in an attempt to protect your feelings.

When your personality is challenged or feels under appreciated, you can hide your work because you feel that your creativity has been stifled. So, why bother to show what you are really capable of doing? The soul wishes you to be the one who appreciates you and causes you to feel content. It is a challenge when you feel everything so deeply to become at peace with your feelings and to integrate them into your life. Yet, that is what the soul wishes to be done, for the soul wishes your emotions not to control your life experiences, instead feelings are to be used as a tool in understanding life.

The goal in the Piscean Age was to feel and sense things without getting lost in illusion or getting swept away with emotions. You are here to finish having those experiences, to learn to put emotions into balance, to see how feelings can be beneficial without dominating your experiences and to learn how not to be manipulated by your feelings. An exercise to see how well you are doing in this department is to listen to, and to analyze, a politician's speech as most use emotional language, not facts, in an attempt to sway people to vote for them. In other words, your soul wishes you to use and enjoy your feelings, without your feelings causing you to forget to use your mind's reasoning abilities.

You prefer life that is in constant motion. Your quest for excitement generates curiosity. You are happy to travel and go places to attend parties and gatherings with others. You seek excitement to have life be less boring; thus, you delve into other people's stories and play the sleuth to figure out what motivates and excites others.

This is because you crave all aspects of beauty and wish the world to be a more beautiful place. This translates into noticing how others dress, if there is a picture that is hanging on the wall crooked, or if the color scheme is monochromatic. This is because your soul wishes to have physical experiences. There is a common saying that goes something like, "You are a spiritual being who came here to learn how to be physical." This applies to you more than any other first vowel. So, enjoy the tastes, textures and physical pleasures available by having a physical body. Your soul wishes to have as many physical experiences as possible without getting lost in physical pleasures where you emphasize them over your spiritual growth.

Your soul wishes for you to experience life through your own adventures and to take in life by way of other's escapades; hence, you are a great listener. You have a great ability to really hear what others are saying as well as what they are not saying. You like to know what the real story is so that you are a natural detective, being able to get to the root cause of situations.

You do not put up with half-truths, so in your detective work, you will notice when something doesn't quite feel right or when facts just don't fit quite right within a story.

To sum up your soul's intent when you have the first vowel of 'E', it is to learn to peel off all emotional feelings, after thoroughly experiencing them, as truth has no feelings, no considerations, and no interpretations. Truth just is. Remember, when your soul is confronted with too many things that are hard for you to digest, your soul is sad and will rebel insofar as you feel separate from yourself. Then selfishness begins. To avoid this destructive path, your soul wishes for you to see the perfect human in you and to develop into it. It is a struggle, but absolutely possible to conquer the demons of humiliation of ego and self-destructive habits.

Remember, Light is…there is nothing to be added. Your soul is endless and para-defined so that in an earthly life, it looks for excitement and pleasures as it feels limited and starved of light. Enjoy life, while learning how to appropriately use emotions and feelings to help you navigate your experiences here. Your soul asks that you put your feelings into proper perspective without being carried away by them.

FIRST VOWEL IS 'I'

When you have the first vowel of 'I', you have come into this lifetime to resolve issues dealing with karma, issues with other people, and especially, issues with family members. You are here to learn how to synchronize with others without losing your individuality or minimizing your self-determining will. Your childhood helped create scenarios that would need resolutions in order to facilitate your own spiritual growth. So, a major growth occurs when you learn how to resolve issues from your original family, situations that were upsetting for you as a child. You could feel that you are responsible for other family members and that it may be necessary to play the mediator. Issues with family may include unresolved feelings of abandonment or ill treatment in childhood, like not getting enough attention while a child.

Your soul craves to be included and to be honored by others. This stems from a lack of recognition while a youth mainly from your family unit. Did your parents portray the idea that you were not good enough? Did you feel like you had to please your parents and that this task was difficult to accomplish or never lasted long enough? This need for inclusivity and approval can also show up as the need to rescue others. Does your need to be needed out weigh your need to be happy?

Regardless of the remaining issues, you must find a way to let it go by engaging forgiveness. Only by forgiving can you create the happiness in your life that you seek. That is because, only by forgiving, can you move forward on the path you came to walk. So, let us redefine the word forgiveness. Forgiveness is the willingness to give back to Creation the problem to be solved. You are for, not against, giving back the situation to be worked out spiritually.

Forgiveness has nothing to do with forgetfulness. You are neither to forget the learning that came with the experience nor to allow someone to use or abuse you again. However, it is vital not to carry sadness, guilt, shame, resentment or any other emotion that originated due to a situation with another person, as it stifles your own life energy and keeps you from claiming what your soul designed as your destiny for you in this incarnation. Your soul wishes for you to learn how to forgive others, as in doing so, you shall learn how to forgive yourself for your part in the situations.

You are rarely satisfied with your ability to communicate clearly or exactly what it is that you intended to say due to your upbringing. Should you express yourself or not? You can talk someone's ear off and then clam up the next day feeling bad about over expressing yourself. You can kick yourself after conversations on what you did or didn't say, or overanalyze what actually was said.

Why are you not connecting with the other person when you are expressing yourself to the best of your ability? When you are not connecting with another person, even as the desire is there, it is your soul saying that this other person is not on your path. Go find the people that you can communicate with clearly as you are here to share your understandings with them.

Others are not ready for your truths yet. Your soul wishes to share your knowledge with those that can hear what it is that you have to say.

You are a natural leader, albeit an idealistic one, and are called to make this world a better place. Yet you can have a lack of confidence in the validity of your desires or even if you have the right to have your desires of being a leader and helping others to feel fulfilled. Please do not feel bad about taking care of yourself or using family resources to do so as the reason you are taking care of yourself is so that you may then take care of others. There will come a time in your life when you are almost forced to make a choice: are you going to lead or miss your opportunity to make a significant difference in the lives of many? Since you enjoy being the focal point, why not lead? Others find it easy to approach you and ask questions or for help. Why not take advantage of this ability of yours to help people feel relaxed around you to make a difference in their lives? You take your role as a leader seriously because it is what gives you purpose and value.

You prefer harmony and work hard at maintaining a sense of serenity, and you don't usually handle anger well regardless if it's your anger or someone else's. Your personality needs to be competent at your job, even on the rare occasions when you are not. Your greatest challenge is not to become 'me first' oriented, self-absorbed or self-centered. If you choose to put yourself first you shall get off track and miss the reason you were here. Your soul wishes for you to use your life experiences, mingled with the depths of feelings that may often go unexpressed, to help others gain a sense of self and the peace that accompanies knowing yourself well. Your soul wants you to know you well, so that you can unselfishly assist your family, friends and neighbors.

FIRST VOWEL IS 'O'

Your soul has a great desire to be needed, and to feel useful which leads you to assisting others as much as possible. You need this as much as the people you help because nothing else fills you up like someone else's gratitude for your help. Without this appreciation factor, you can feel empty as if something is missing in your life. Thus, you find your fulfillment in assisting others. Remember, the way you assist can actually hinder the other person's growth. Find people that are already on their path and help them get where they are going faster than they could have done so by going it alone. In other words, help those that are helping themselves to grow and learn.

The disdain that you feel when you are nagged is the quiet voice within stating that you are not good enough. Your thoughts say that others would not nag you if you were a more worthwhile person. Thus, doubt is created within your being. Instead of looking within and recognizing your own growing disillusionment with the outer world, you tend to make the nagger wrong so that you can continue to live within the illusion that all is perfect just the way it is.

Your greatest challenge is to look to God or Creation for security and not to look to others or the almighty dollar. You may find yourself apologizing for your outbursts of temper, self-assertion or even statements of want due to your lack of knowing that your desires deserve to be manifested. So, it is important to learn to accept your own desires and feelings of anger as valid so that feelings can be expressed in an honest and outright manner with confidence.

You enjoy telling others what to do, so that you may exhibit the experience that you would like to have; however you don't wish to incorporate the result of that experience unless you know it will go well. So, by telling others what to do, you can watch what happens to them prior to deciding if that is the way you would also like to go. Since you are able to multitask well and love telling others what to do, you are good at being in charge and happy when you are your own boss. At the very least, you need autonomy in what you do. Your soul learns by leading and taking care of others, so you can be a great boss when you incorporate your soul's care taking intent.

The good news is that you have the potential to be a fabulous parent, and your children are lucky to have you parent them even when they don't realize it. Remember, sometimes it takes time for children to realize the gains they made due to your great parenting skills. As much as you like to be appreciated and acknowledged by others, realize that not until your children have children will they appreciate your parenting style. Your soul's intent while you are parenting is to learn to listen and learn from your children while not becoming too bossy. Since you don't like being told what to do, this can be a great challenge. Often you will have at least one child who is here to teach you, so the learning is mutual and not just from parent to child.

Your soul's goal of nurturing others is apparent in how you treat your coworkers and your family. Your soul is a bright one and has magnetic energy that draws people to you. Your soul's hope is that you will use this magnetism wisely to educate others and not to take advantage of them.

In the emotional realm, your soul wishes you to experience loyalty and the lack thereof. The reason for this is that lack of loyalty towards you causes you to hold a grudge, and your soul wishes you to learn how to accept others as they are with all of their imperfections. Thus when people are disloyal, you are given an opportunity to accept them with all of their perceived shortcomings. It is important for your soul to see limitations as temporary and non-crucial and to be able to forgo a grudge.

Your challenge is not to bury your head in the sand and think that as long as you do not discuss negative challenges, they do not exist. You handle the day-to-day problems well, but what about what is happening around you in the world? Can you see reality clearly or are you more comfortable existing within your sacred, rose-colored, bubble? It is important to hear differing viewpoints, even those that cause you to feel uncomfortable, so that you can live in a world acknowledging what is actually happening versus your view of what is happening. The challenge is to stay open to outside viewpoints, of all flavors, and not to simply surround yourself with others that feel the exact same way that you do. Said another way, it is important not to bury your head in the sand, but instead to stretch your neck out like a giraffe to see a wider view.

Another challenge for you is not to evaluate how much you are loved by how many material possessions you are given, for love cannot be equated with anything material. Love is honestly appreciating another person's essence, not having another person spend a lot of money on you. So, your soul wants you to realize that the people who love you the most are probably not the same ones who are using their finances to buy your affection. Ask yourself who has really been there for you when needed, the one with the open pocketbook or the one who supported you with time, with their listening skills and with their knowledge?

Lastly, your soul wishes for you to see the value in routine and in the willingness to forgo routine as well as knowing when to change routines. Your soul is usually happiest when boundaries are clear and consistent as that is when maximum growth occurs for you.

FIRST VOWEL IS 'U'

You came to experience a joyous life and can easily become depressed when life is not so or life does not live up to your expectations. Your soul desires to experience creativity in all of its many manifestations. Thus, you often become an entertainer, or at the very least, have fascinating conversations. You are here to promote laughter, clear communication, and the need for story telling. Early in life you are reminded of this need to be creative, as your creativity most often has been stifled as a child. You are normally animated and enthusiastic. Your soul wishes for you to remember to be genuine, to lighten up and to get more enjoyment out of life by not taking life so seriously. Thus, you can be quite playful. Children expect to learn and are innocent in their initial approaches to learning. Your soul wants to remind adults to do the same: that we are not expected to necessarily succeed on the first try and that learning can be enjoyable, valuable, naturally occurring and worth seeking.

Being an entertainer and someone who loves to have fun, you may instigate change in others just to keep from being bored. You are the natural chameleon, as you will adapt yourself to your surroundings and can make the best out of any situation as long as you feel you are effective in your endeavors.

Your soul constantly reminds you to "let go and let God" do the work. Said another way, it is as if God said, "Good morning. This is God. I will be handling all your problems today. I will not need your help. So, have a good day." Your soul wishes to have fun, to enjoy life, to spread harmony and wisdom that comes from the deeper levels of your life. There is so much to be unraveled to bring forth the diamonds that are needed in your world to see there is still much glory to be found. The real challenge is to enjoy the diamonds, without needing to have them.

Your challenge is not to need to be the center of attention, or to exaggerate to get wanted attention nor to relish being in the spotlight to satisfy your need for attention. Your true nature is feeding on what spirit is giving you. Spirit is not that glamorous and will not give you glory and recognition; it will simply add to your soul life and happiness.

You are here to remind the rest of humanity to live in the moment, in the present time zone, and not to dwell too much on either the past or the future for now is all anyone has. Your soul is here to demonstrate what delicious love looks and feels like. To assist your soul accomplish its mission, it is important that you stay focused on doing what you think is best in the long run for the people with whom you are interacting without attempting to control the outcome. You are sharing what love you have. Your soul also wishes you to realize that needing to be in control or in charge of the ones you love is not love. Guiding others, offering suggestions, and appreciating who they are is love; not making unwanted decisions for the ones you love. Your soul asks, 'Can you love unconditionally or do you set up conditions?" You know that unconditional love is your aim.

FIRST VOWEL IS 'Y'

The 'Y' vowel works a bit differently than the other vowels due to the fact that sometimes 'Y' is considered a vowel and other times it is not. If you have the 'Y' as the first vowel in your name then you are most happy when working on the spiritual side of your life. You are here to investigate an array of beliefs usually outside normal parameters. You would benefit from a regular spiritual practice, be it meditation, prayer work, reading inspired writings or simply sitting in silence and reflecting. You have a strong inner voice that is in a constant inner dialogue. Give yourself permission to question what you see and hear, especially as it relates to religious teachings, as you are one who needs to have your own experiences, and not rely on the experiences of another. This accounts for you being a realist. Thus, it is important for you to continually have new experiences.

Your challenge is not to get into a rut such that you stop exploring new ideas or stop having new adventures. Your soul wishes you to continually explore the spiritual side of religions. It is important not to get stuck in one religion or to ever think you have found a definitive answer about our Creator. Instead, explore the different facets of varying faiths to find out exactly what works for you. Imagine all of the different possible religions as ingredients in a pie. You stir them all together and then pour them into the pie pan. You let the pie cook, stimulating the various ideas in your head. You let the pie cool, which is similar to letting the ideas percolate and settle in yourself. Finally, you cut a slice from the pie, and whatever beliefs were in that slice are the ideas that you accept. Thus, you glean ideas from all religions, and yet belong or endorse none of them.

You are a tremendous observer of humans and are able to see the extremes of human behaviors as well as everything in between. Witnessing so much drama, and being able to see all sides of a situation has allowed you to make better choices about your own behavior. Thus, you observe a situation before making any conclusions.

The one outstanding behavior that bothers you is another person's rudeness. When you see what you interpret to be rudeness on the part of another person, you plan your revenge. Being a gracious host, you would never cause a scene to occur; however, that doesn't stop you from starting to plot the rude person's comeuppance. However long it takes, whenever the right situation should present itself, you will even the score.

The challenge here is to remember that, 'Vengeance is mine, saith the Lord". This is to be taken seriously, for even as it is difficult not to consider revenge, it is highly important not to act on those thoughts. Even if you witness the person's comeuppance, and do not have to plan it yourself, it is not yours to take pleasure in seeing someone else minimized.

Be aware when you become overbearing or overpowering when not getting your own way. You have a lethal tongue and can be highly destructive when mad. You make a dangerous enemy, especially due to your desire to retaliate regardless of how long the wait or the number of details needed to execute the perfect plan. Remember, you are here to learn to trust the universe to make things right and you do not have to take vengeance into your own hands. Now, this does not mean when you see an obvious injustice to not do anything and not to say anything. Stating an opinion, standing up to bullies, and letting your position be known is appropriate; however, seeking revenge and damages to another through willful acts of your own, when you initiate, is not appropriate.

You want justice and find it difficult to live with what you perceive to be injustices. However, that does not mean it is your job to make it right. Remember, you are probably totally unaware of the circumstances that took place prior to the incident that you witnessed. So, you are not seeing the whole picture nor understanding the motivations behind the actions. Also, you are looking at the situation through your own filtered lenses. Let life be the redeemer.

Make peace within yourself as you were meant to be a creator and not meant to be a warrior. Besides, you are here to learn how to consistently evaluate others clearly as your judgment can be clouded by politics, peer pressure and your own desires. Sentiments can also play a big role in how you feel about others, even as you have learned how to convincingly hide your emotions from others.

You are here to assist others get beyond their fears and be willing to try new things. You are here to creatively solve the most complex of problems using both your wondrous ability to think outside the norm and your precociousness.

You are not here to insist that your way of

seeing something is absolutely the best way possible. Instead, it is to explore all options so that you can realize new truths.

Above all other first vowels, you have the ability to be gracious, which causes others to feel welcomed and included. This is what you came to share with others along with your high intellect. For whatever field excites you, you become an expert in that field. Share with others, be gracious and enjoy divergent experiences. That is what makes a successful life for you.

ALL VOWELS PRESENT IN A NAME

You came to learn how to effectively communicate with everyone else. No one is beyond your capability to communicate clearly with people and to be able to help each of them see themselves better. You are able to see everyone's point of view; thus, you can help others see another's point of view and not be stuck in their own visions. Having all the vowels in your name indicates that you are here in service to individuals in this world. Your greatest challenge is to focus your energy as you are talented in so many different areas that it can be difficult to focus on just one thing.

CHAPTER 3:
FIRST LETTER IN FIRST NAME

"Yesterday is history. Tomorrow is mystery. Today is a gift." Eleanor Roosevelt

The first letter in the first name represents the spiritual challenges that are most easily recognized in your name. This letter indicates how to bring balance into your life with both challenges and gifts. The first letter is gives the first impression as it indicates your nature, how you approach situations and what is most important to you.

Remember those with a multiplicity of gifts must figure out how to use them all so that none are wasted; where much is given, much is expected. The first letter brings you the modality or energy that is available to you. The challenges in this letter represent where you need to be humbled to grow or where your ego may be out of control; whereas, the gifts in the letter are those qualities that you are here to share with others. Remember, this is the pathway that was decided prior to you coming into physicality.

We all continue to grow as long as we accept the tests that life gives to us and remain honest in our endeavors. However, we cannot discern truth when we get caught up in fear to the extent that fear rules us. As long as we seek truth and are honest, darkness and fears will never gain control over us. They may try but are doomed to failure. It takes great courage to live the truth, especially now while so many are living in ignorance and allowing their fears to rule them. However, we are living in a great time when many are waking up daily to the joys of consciousness and are ready to celebrate other people.

We may find ourselves giving our fears more power than our faith can withstand, and therefore, need to change our current course. It is all right to change course as long as it is done with love and truth. With faith comes sensitivity which leads to clarity, and that is what leads us to knowing what our next steps in life are to be and what course is appropriate to take.

Just as religions are based on the truth yet stray into dogma, outside authority is attempting to help us but is most often used to control people. People with power issues, those that have not found it within themselves to see that all are equally important to Creation and all have value, crave authority. This is because they fail to see their own worth accurately, or they allow their fears to rule them. In order to hide these fears or to invalidate them, power hungry people are the ones that attempt to control others so that they can feel better about themselves. These are the people who seek power over others, and simultaneously, are most afraid of other people.

If each of us could learn to think for ourselves or gain the understanding that we can learn on our own while maintaining our faith in the connection of all people, then, we as individuals, would be extremely dangerous to power seeking individuals as we would be naturally powerful. Imposed power, be it from governments, religions, or any institution, has no effect on people who can think for themselves and who choose to understand other people and treat them with compassion. Thus, the desire for understanding and the intention of compassion are the keys to liberating oneself from the grasp of the beast who wishes to control others out of fear. Remember, all heinous acts are the result of fear. All disparaging acts are caused by fears. Do not be afraid, allowing yourself to be controlled by another out of fear of your physical body, for as Robert Monroe [17] teaches, we are much more than our physical bodies.

Not all people who are allowing fear to dominate their lives need to exercise power over others. For these people, when fear is stronger than faith, the fear manifests into illness and disease. Fear creates all diseases and ailments

---

[17] Robert Monroe coined the term OBE for "out of body" experiences and founded the Monroe Institute. He has written three books documenting out of body experiences and what was learned from these including the fact that we are more than our physical bodies. In fact, the sentence, " we are more than our physical bodies" is ingrained into his prayers. In the face of full disclosure, the author is a trained, certified outreach trainer with the Monroe Institute.

that one does not have when born whether the person is aware of this or not. If you do not live in fear in the mind, then you will keep yourself healthy in body and soul as healthy thought patterns places layers of healing protection throughout and around one's body. When fear or darkness enters your being, you create a space that allows ailments to grow. One can control any disease of the mind or body once fear has been conquered. Remember not to fear for one self as all is well in Creation.

Marianne Williamson[18] wrote that to receive a miracle one must first believe in miracles. Billy Grimsley, in his paper on miracles defined a miracle as a shift in self-perception.[19] If you do not believe in miracles and if you do not believe you can be healed or that things can change, then everything will stay the same as it is currently. Only when we accept the thought that we co-create what occurs in our lives, will we also accept the responsibility of changing that which we do not like. All things are possible within Creation. The first letter in the first name identifies some of our greatest fears and how to grow through that particular fear.

---
18 Author of A Course in Miracles
19 Miracles; A Shift in Perception by Billy Grimsley

FIRST LETTER IS 'A'

The letter 'A' is one of the more spiritual letters in the alphabet. The more 'A's you have in your name, the more energy there is for spiritual understanding and a thirst to learn new spiritual concepts. Think of Paramahansa Yogananda, author of Autobiography of a Yogi, the great Eastern Spiritual teacher who opened up the west to eastern ideas by introducing meditation and other eastern practices.

When the first letter of your first name is 'A' you have a tendency to work hard in order to get other people's approval. Thus, your challenge is to learn to approve of yourself and not to expect to receive from another that which is held internally within yourself. Your soul seeks peace; yet, you are one whose inner peace can be disturbed by another's criticism of you. You often allow yourself to be unnecessarily concerned with another person's opinion of you. Your challenge in this life is to discover how to approve of yourself so that you can maintain the inner peace your soul craves.

FIRST LETTER IS 'B'

If the first letter of your name is 'B', you are highly competitive and judge yourself from how much and how often you win. This causes wounds to develop when you are beaten by another or didn't come out on top. The challenge for you is to heal old wounds and not to carry them with you. Not everything is a competition, so your goal is to discover how to cherish your relationships with others and not to let old wounds get in the way. Focusing on past events will cause you to have a more difficult time in this life than people whose name starts with any other letter. Your soul's goal for you in this lifetime is for you to use your winning drive into creating situations where everyone wins. Your soul craves companionship and solid relationships, and creating as many win-win situations as possible is the way to achieve that goal.

Your fear is that you are not good enough, and thus, you make sure that you are better than others in something that eases your competitive nature. If you don't think you will be good enough at doing something, you often will not even try to do it eliminating any possibility of failure. This need to prove your worth, that you are indeed good enough, drives your motivations and choices. Think how much of life you are missing out on when not experiencing new things for fear of failure. Once you can accept that no one is good at everything and can allow yourself not to be afraid of failure, you have conquered the challenge in this letter. Then you can enjoy being the best without ever doubting that you are not good enough.

FIRST LETTER IS 'C'

When your name starts with the letter 'C' you can be charming and charismatic to cover your need to be in charge and in control. Your natural charm disarms others into letting you lead, besides, you know things will turn out better when you are the leader. You also know how to keep secrets.

This need to be in control causes you also to

need to be right at all costs. Friendships can be lost over this need to be right and not being able to admit mistakes. What is not realized here is the need to be right or the ultimate authority on what is best, disallows others in your company the joy of sharing with you, of helping you along your path. The need to be right alienates you from others without you being able to realize how you have contributed to others not wanting to include you. This is a difficult lesson to learn for the soul and yet an important one. You have come to learn how to apologize, how to admit mistakes and how to let go of that which you cannot control. Your most favorite saying is, "I am always right regardless of how wrong I appear."

When you feel you are losing control of yourself and/or your situations is when you feel the most need to control others. and so, acting out of fear, you do your best to control the people around you, or at the very least, control the situations around you so that you will feel safe. Your life becomes more joyous in direct proportion to your ability to trust and allow situations and people to be what and who they are.

The bottom line on what you came to learn is to trust that all has a purpose in the Universe so that you don't need to control things to make them come out right. Your challenge is to so trust in a Higher Power that there is no need to walk in fear. This way you give the eternal Light within you a chance to grow brighter. Then, and only then, will your bondages of fear be released. Also, that is when others benefit the most from you being in the lead.

FIRST LETTER IS 'D'

When your first name begins with 'D', your salvation lies in using your imagination in creative endeavors. You will often have clutter around you as a messy environment is the key to starting the ignition to your creativity. One of the challenges in your name is to discover how to limit your clutter to chosen areas, so that your area doesn't become one huge clutter pile.

You arrived on earth with a strong connection to the divine regardless if it is acknowledged or not. Your challenge is not to walk in fear so that the eternal light within you can glow and grow and continue to shine brighter as time passes. As you allow your light to shine, all those bondages of fear shall be released. Once you acknowledge the glow within you, you are preordained to be able to assist others simply with your presence. Words will not be needed to convey the love in your heart and the connection that you hold. When others inquire what makes you glow the way you do, the words will come as well as the love for both of you. Your challenge is to allow your divinity to shine through clearly without getting tangled up with fear concerning worldly chaos. Let your light shine and be an example to those around you so that they too find it safe to shine.

'D' is the divine letter as it signifies your soul connection to the Divine and that you are always supported. Your soul started out connected, is currently connected and, will always remain connected. You may feel that you have gone off path at different times, but it is not true. Your soul guides you continuously. Your challenge is to figure out how to strengthen your divine connection and to use it to assist others as your joy is relative to both your knowingness and your comfort level being guided by your soul.

FIRST LETTER IS 'E'

Those of you whose name starts with the letter 'E' are fortunate as you are a detective and have wonderful listening skills. You already know that your soul is connected to the oneness principle; you just know things about others. Your challenges are to be willing to explore that which appears strange or unusual and for you to be comfortable with people who disagree with you. You find your comfort with those of like mind even when it limits your own awareness, and in spite of your natural curiosity, of others who are different from yourself. Your soul is the explorer, and as such, requires tremendous amounts of social interaction.

You will have fulfilled a major goal in your life when you are able to see your faults, and those of others, without judgment or becoming depressed. You often feel burdened. In response, you live your life in the extremes. You either live in the future, full of dreams and focusing on the thrills that life has to offer, thus being frivolous, living like your life will never end, or you live in the past commiserating all past miseries. Your life purpose is double fold. First is to be present, fully attentive in the now, and appreciating what life has to offer you. Your second purpose is to discover how to see yourself and others clearly, warts and all. Your soul does not care if others agree or disagree with you. Can you get your personality to agree with your soul? That is the challenge and what you came to learn.

FIRST LETTER IS 'F'

In one respect you have a definite challenge when your name begins with 'F', which is balanced with a tremendous gift. First for the challenge, your soul has come to experience honesty and to realize that dishonesty hurts you as much as it does others. It is important to distinguish the difference and the minutia that honesty requires. For example, did you tell yourself that you would only play one more hole of golf before going home, but then played more than that? Did you promise yourself to get up at a certain hour and when the alarm goes off and you push the snooze button? These are small promise to yourself, but important ones all the same. You came to learn extreme honesty as you lead others, and it is important to use that influence in a positive manner. You have the amazing ability to be the Tom Sawyer in your area: to get others to do your work for you. You came into this life this time around to develop and to perfect your integrity.

You have a fabulous imagination that is a strong creative tool. However, how you picture things to be is never quite the way things turn out to be which leaves you wondering what happened. You came to give and to receive and when one of these two parts is out of balance, then, your creative imagination proves faulty. You came to use your vivid imagination to create for the good of the whole where everyone benefits, not just a few or just yourself. When any form of selfishness enters the picture, you will find nothing but disappointments, as your triumphs will be short lived. This can also be said when you give too much of yourself to others. One of your missions is to learn how to balance yourself between giving to and receiving from others.

FIRST LETTER IS 'G'

Gee, the 'G's are adventuresome and can become addicted to physical pleasures. Your soul came to experience as many different experiences as possible without taking any one experience to the extreme. Through your adventures you learn about life and observe life and thus learn from the inside out like how something cooks in the microwave oven. People with 'G' for a first initial came to be flexible and demonstrate how to gracefully adjust to change. However, they will often find it more comfortable to live within a flexible routine versus having no routine at all. Yet, you have come to learn to be able to adjust as quickly as possible and to help others to do so also.

You get bored easily as your soul learns what it needs from your experiences and then wants to move forward. You are encouraged by art, beauty and creativity. Follow your heart and curb your addictions to people and substances and your soul will be thrilled. People who have a name starting with 'G' can easily become addicted, so you came to experience life without getting too attached to anything.

Change and flexibility are difficult for most and yet you crave it, just as you crave authority over others even as you deny both of these needs. You seek change to force you to remain open to the divine light that you are. You seek authority when you live in fear of knowing yourself too clearly. Your challenge is to stay strong in your faith so that it may conquer your fears. When your faith is strong, you radiate. Once that starts, you don't even need words to know that change is occurring in others around you as you have now provided a safe environment for changes to take place. People will gravitate toward you and question you. In their asking, you will know that you are being of service to someone and your need to be the authority shall vanish. May your faith be ever strong and your fears few.

FIRST LETTER IS 'H'

You came to be made aware of human possibilities. You are the same as others, and yet, you hold light and that light causes you to be lucky. Thus, you can royally screw up and yet always land on you feet or as the saying goes, come out smelling like a rose. Garbage does not stick to you. Therefore, you can leave a bad situation and not have it affect you in your next environment.

You are here to become aware of human possibilities and share those possibilities with others. It is important for you to understand that everyone is one as all stem from the Creator, and in Creation, it is all one great life. The important thing for you to remember is to live through your heart, to be of service and care for others while maintaining balance that you and others are the same. There are no differences as you all have equal value in Creation.

'H' is the holy letter as it is easy to simply go with the flow of whatever is occurring around you. Since it is so easy to go with the flow, it can be a challenge to stay motivated or to go against the stream of what is popular or consider something other than your own preconceived ideas. Your soul wishes for you to use your ease of being to assist others by encouraging them in their own endeavors. The challenge for you is to stay focused on assisting others versus simply focusing on yourself as things come easily for you. Thus, by helping others to find the joy in life, you find it yourself. Yours is a path of selfless service in humility. When this path is followed, everyone around you benefits including yourself. Any service which is motivated by selfishness, or for your own gain, ends up in disaster for it is against your own soul's purpose for this lifetime.

FIRST LETTER IS 'I'

Inclusivity is the key word for souls who chose to start their name with the letter 'I'. Your soul wishes for you to include others just as much as you wish to be included. Your challenge is to forgo the need to be the leader, not that you cannot be the leader, but not to be the leader to satisfy your need for the attention that a leader commands. You can work for yourself or choose to fully support your boss, if working for another. It is highly important for you to learn not to undermine other leaders in any way, especially your bosses as that implies you are here for your own egoic needs.

You like to be included and wish to be asked to join the activity even when it is well known that you don't like that particular activity. You still wish to be asked to know that you are being considered and are desirable. This stems from a feeling of not being wanted and/or wanting to fit in with the other people around you. In other words, you wish to feel loved by being included. Your soul wishes you to know that you are loved regardless of whether others include you or not. You have value regardless if others see it or not. Your soul wishes you to know that you are the one who needs to value you. Simply enjoy it when others love and value you without needing them to do so. Remember that when you are feeling the need to be needed, it is only because you are temporarily forgetting your own value. Other people readily feel comfortable around you. Isn't that enough confirmation that you have value?

Your soul is here this lifetime to balance both the need to receive and the need to give, and to monitor your own needs, just as you monitor the needs of others so that neither gets out of balance. You are here to enjoy life by living it to the fullest and assisting others to do the same.

FIRST LETTER IS 'J'

The natural brilliance of the souls who have chosen to have a name that begins with 'J' is astounding. This is because these souls have ancient knowledge from those days so long ago. Having such ancient knowledge is both a blessing and a curse. With such a vast reservoir of knowledge, your soul can foresee things, sense things, and can see the result of current actions before the results happen. You feel that everyone is like you, and yet, that is not the case at all resulting in your soul feeling restless.

Before age thirty, you have multiple challenges such as how do you handle being intuitive while simultaneously not acknowledging your own intuition? Frequently, you either do not honor your own inner wisdom or persecute yourself for having inner knowledge as it makes you feel different from others, and you long to belong. These challenges start to dissipate during your thirties as you begin to acknowledge that without your intuition your soul would be lost.

You came in with a heightened sense of intuitiveness. However, this may also scare you as how do you know the things you know? This intuitive sense is to aid you to walk your own path, to create your own beliefs, and not to be a sheep and follow the crowd.

You came to learn how to follow your own lead. You may ask others their opinion, or garner information from outside sources like books and the Internet, but ultimately, you are not to repeat what has come before you. You are here to take the path less traveled and in so doing forge a new pathway for others to use. It is acceptable to try on different modes, to see how they fit as long as your do not lose yourself in one of these modes.

Often, you forget that you are here to lead, and so, you lower your own vibration through alcohol, or other substances, in order to fit in with those around you better. Remember that you take yourself off path when you drink or do drugs in an attempt to fit in better with others socially. This is a veiled attempt to dumb yourself down so that you match the ones around you which is both harmful to your physicality and does not really even work. You came to think for yourself and to be yourself regardless of your ability to fit in with others.

Thus, with all of your soul's ancient knowledge, you are here to lead others and help them through the problems that you so readily know how to solve. Your greatest challenge is not to deny your own soul's direction nor yield to someone else's vision that is imposed upon you. You so wish to belong and get along with those that are less knowledgeable than you are that you leave your own path which you know to be right for you to fit in with others. Instead, your soul urges you to follow your own inner urges for you are the wise men and women of the current age and are precious gems in this world.

FIRST LETTER IS 'K'

You came to learn how to use power effectively and fairly for a part of you has feared or misused power in the past. You are not to lord your power over another but instead use it to guide others in how to use their power wisely. Your challenge is not to fear powerful people, for you are comfortable with material power and are here to learn to be comfortable with spiritual power. Do not fear those who have this type of power for they are not threats to you. Instead let their use of spiritual power define and guide your use of material power. You are a competent businessperson. Allow that gift of authority to be used well in leading and guiding others. Your challenge is not to allow power to define you and to rule you or to be scared of losing that power. Remember, force will not get you where you choose to be. No one can take your power from you. Instead, recognize that you hold power within you, and it cannot be lost.

You who have 'K' for the first letter of your name have a soul who wants to lead for the benefit of all financially. You came to experience prosperity and what the world has to offer and to share that prosperity with those whom you love, both family, friends and colleagues. Your soul's challenge is not to get frustrated, or even angry, when your dreams take a bit longer to manifest than what you want or when others cannot read your mind to do what you are wanting in the time you are expecting. You must be careful not to destroy yourself from within with your anger that can easily turn into rage. Your soul is a leader of the finest variety for as you learn to encourage others, you also learn how to foster your own inner creativity and happiness. Furthermore, as you learn to take care of others, you also learn how to take care of yourself more responsibly. Your soul carries an extra challenge as you must learn to cherish yourself without the need to prove who you are or your worth to others. Through prosperity and enjoying your life, your soul learns to love itself and life.

FIRST LETTER IS 'L'

Everyone is afraid of something. We are all afraid. The trick is to acknowledge our fears so that we can learn to walk into them, thus learning not to be afraid. The fear that accompanies the letter 'L' is fear of people and what they might do to you. You came in with an abundance of self-confidence, and then allowed yourself to be influenced by others whereas making it possible for you to lose your greatest asset. Do not compare yourself to others, for there will always be those that are ahead of you and those that are behind you in understanding.

Remember, you walk with our Creator, and that spark grows within you. It does not come from outside of you. You have the ability to carry the eternal Light in your heart when fear is not present. Everyone is attracted to those with self-confidence. Your challenge is to allow your self-confidence to shine, without affectations, and to live the brightness of your spirit without letting others dampen your spirit.

You souls who lead your lives with the letter 'L' are here to learn to appreciate the physicality and not to punish yourselves for your own hardships that you tend to bring upon yourselves. You bring confidence into this world with you, and then, must learn how to keep it.

Your soul is enterprising and wants to be recognized and thus must learn to care for others as well as self. Your challenge is to include others even when your independence is screaming to do it yourself. You came here to give positive reinforcement to others and not to tear others down when they get in the way of you achieving what you came to do.

FIRST LETTER IS 'M'

This is an interesting letter as either you are manipulative and a bit self-centered or you bring numerous people around you who are manipulative and a bit self-centered, so that you get to learn from these characteristics from either the sending side or the receiving side. You came to learn to have no expectations on what life is supposed to be. You must learn to have faith without arrogance, without being obnoxious, without needing others *f*to support you.

Souls who begin their name with the letter 'M' are intense so they must learn to discern what is needed and what is not; what to keep and what no longer serves. The 'M' soul is concerned with self first and others second, thus they form habits, which can be difficult to break, as they don't listen well to others outside of themselves. They must learn to appreciate their bodies and not abuse the body with unhealthy choices.

Often these souls are rescuers, or enablers, as they must be seen as the 'good guy'. They can play 'poor pity me' well to seduce others into sharing the other's resources, or they simply take what they feel is rightfully theirs, even when it is not. The challenge of the 'M' is plentiful. 'M's must learn how to heal their own wounds first, afterwards the 'M' will frequently turn his knowledge into a healing art to be shared with others. The 'M' soul can have inner turmoil when it finally decides to confront their thoughts on entitlement.

You did not come here to depend on others; only to depend on yourself. As you heal from scars obtained in other time, you will learn to love others the same as you love yourself. This great healing, once accomplished, will open all the doors you have always craved to be open. Remember, you must acknowledge your temptation to think yourself better than others and allow your heart to open so that entitlement and arrogance do not find a nesting place within you.

Be grateful for what is shared with you as no one owes you anything. When others share with you it is coming from their hearts. This is to be appreciated and not expected. Opening the heart is not a quick process. Then, and only then, will Creation's kingdom will be open to you.

This is a difficult letter in the first letter position. You must learn to have faith and compassion for others so that others will have the same for you. That is how you get ahead this lifetime. Remember, doors will open for you as you learn that others are equally as important as you are.

FIRST LETTER IS 'N'

Souls who have names that start with 'N' are waiting for life to find them versus going out and seeking life. These souls enjoying 'flying by the seat of their pants' and wish to keep seeking that which is new versus dwelling on the past. The challenge for the 'N' is to not get bogged down in minutia, so that they can continue to see each day as if this is the first day of their life. It is easier for you to see the details than the whole picture. So, a challenge for you is to be able to step back and see the whole picture and how your details work together to make up the whole. Said another way, you are not supposed to get so focused on the details that the larger picture totally escapes you.

These souls enjoy order and so they tend to organize and over organize the things and the people around them. They feel the world needs to be conducted in a more orderly fashion. This stems from a fear that the world is not as it should be. The challenge for you, if your name begins with 'N', is to see the world providing exactly what everyone needs in order to grow, thus eliminating the need to complain about how things are versus how things could, should, or would be.

You do better when surrounded by positive versus negative people. So, choose your company wisely and be aware when you are speaking negatively as this can become a bad habit. Your challenge is to find the positive, or the silver lining, in every situation, and not to dwell on the negative. Look for those things where you can make a difference versus spending time on matters that simply frustrate you as you feel disempowered to do anything about the situation. It is extremely important that you focus on the positive by asking: "What is there to learn in this situation? Why did I participate in this situation? What is the silver lining here?" There is always something positive to be gleaned from every experience and it is your job to find it. Staying positive keeps you on path whereas negativity takes you off path.

FIRST LETTER IS 'O'

You, who have the first letter of 'O', are the natural nurturers and full of love for self, for others and for life. Your challenge is not to let life take this grand ability to love away from you. To grow, your soul must learn to parent self and then share your knowledge with others. This is irrelevant as to what kind of parents you had. It is to say that you must develop your own style of parenting that is both nurturing and fair. Thus, you learn first how to love yourselves and then how to share that love with others without losing your sense of self in the process.

Another challenge for you is to be able to

see opposing viewpoints as helpful versus something to be avoided. You are much more comfortable being with people who share your viewpoints than those who do not. In fact, you have taught the people around you what is safe to discuss and what is not. This is part of your innate internal safety program that as long as you are the boss and everyone is doing your bidding, than the world is a safe, or safer, place. The goal here is to be able to assimilate other's viewpoints, and truly listen to their logic, and then to see where the commonality is and whether the other person actually has a valid point. Could another viewpoint be equally as right as your own and yet different? You are here to experience growth through the exploration of ideas, versus being fearful of what may happen if people have different viewpoints than yours.

FIRST LETTER IS 'P'

You who have names that begin with 'P' are

the ones who stand on the shoulders of others. You are the playful ones who come to push others ahead of you and help them build up their enterprises so that they in turn pull you up to a higher level. It is a game of leap frog; you help them get ahead and they help you get ahead. The challenge for you is to allow the other person to go first as you like to rest assured that you will get ahead. This is similar to the game of leapfrog where you alternate who is getting ahead by taking turns jumping over each other. However, you seemingly forget to do your part and help the ones who helped you. Said another way, once you jumped ahead you stopped playing leapfrog.

This can look like borrowing money from parents or older siblings and then never paying your relative back, because, you know, you reason that helping you is their job. Beware of having entitlement issues that somehow you deserve more than others. You have come to learn how to play leapfrog, and to truly share honestly by remembering who helps you and to help them also.

You are here to make others look good while

taking the moral high ground and ensuring others around you do the same. It is not easy for your soul to constantly put others first; yet, your challenge is to learn to put others first and not to be self-centered or selfish.

You are the Pied Piper of souls and so you will lead others to where they wish to go and have a great power of influence. How will you use this power to influence others? It is important that you choose to live to the highest of what you know and encourage others to do so also as it is just as easy to lead others into the gutter as it is to lead them to the top of the mountain. Your challenge is not to take advantage of your ability to persuade others to do your bidding. Instead, use your influence to the best of all concerned utilizing a high ethical code.

FIRST LETTER IS 'Q'

You are the queens or sovereign rulers of the world when your name begins with the letter 'Q'. Your soul wishes to explore the delights that can be found in the mental world and loves chatter and debate. Your challenge is to learn to think before speaking so that others do not overly influence you nor do you accidentally put off others by your presentation method. You can be mighty strong in your opinions and instead of presenting them lightly to others, you want to cram them down a person's throat. "Why can't people just do what they are told?" becomes your motto instead of providing the rational behind your suggestions. Your challenge here is to have patience with those around you who simply do not catch on as quickly as you do, nor process information as quickly as you do. Be generous with your knowledge versus becoming frustrated with the seeming slowness of others. Your soul's challenge is not to become disillusioned, angry or frustrated by other minds who cannot grasp what you wish to express. Thus, the challenge becomes how to cope with others? In order to gain peace with those around you who do challenge your thoughts, you may take the easy road and succumb to living in another's reality instead of your own. Your challenge is to learn to live by your rules while not interfering with the rules that others create for their lives. Can you stay strong in your convictions and beliefs while simultaneously learning how to weave throughout the patterns of life? You have the inner strength and determination to do just that, so the question is, will you?

FIRST LETTER IS 'R'

Your rebellious spirit is an aid in helping you to distinguish the truth from a lie, as you have no tolerance for liars. However, you can fail to see how you are lying to yourself, let alone to others to get what you want done. Your rebelliousness is an asset when it doesn't spread into all categories for it helps you to distinguish the real truth from the current perceived truth. It helps you to think for yourself and not to accept that which you are told unconditionally. Use this asset sparingly so that it does not lead you down the road of resentment. When things don't go your way, there is a tendency to carry resentment about how life is not fair. Your soul wants you to learn how to be sincerely happy for another's success even when you feel it was not deserved. Remember that when the people around you are successful, it is creations way of showing you that you are getting ready to be there also. Observe how others handle success so that you don't gloat over your own when the time comes. Being happy for others is the major lesson here.

You who have souls that chose to begin your name with the letter 'R' are the warriors of truth. You wield a sword and wish to cut everyone's head off that does not share the same understandings that you have so that you feel they have lied. You are a constant truth seeker and must learn how to handle having your beliefs challenged. Your soul is an avenger who wishes to make things right in the world. Your challenge is to realize that you are dominant in the spiritual realm; yet, you are still living in the physical one and must come to peace with that knowledge. Your challenge is also to be sure you ask questions before chopping off someone's head.

FIRST LETTER IS 'S'

You like to keep to a schedule as things flow better for you when you know what is coming. You are great at back-up plans and generally do not like surprises. Your schedule helps keep you get the job done, and so you have a tendency to over schedule yourself, cramming as much as possible into each day or schedule others around you to maximize efficiency. This works in your mind, and yet, sets you up for numerous disappointments. When overwhelmed by your ambitious schedule, you simply start forgetting parts and resort to needing others to rescue and help finish your goals. Part of what you came to learn is how to plan your work, and then, to work your plan so that you can stack up your accomplishments.

The other challenge for the 'S' is the desire to live in physical comfort, to make one's life easier. Thus the focus can be on the physical more than the spiritual. So, how do you live a spiritual life while enjoying physical comforts without allowing the physical needs to overwhelm the spiritual ones? This can be done by giving self a spiritual practice of reading inspired works daily or through a meditation practice, to name a few examples. Once work is planned and a spiritual practice is implemented, you will find yourself in the Creator's service as you are now a dependable initiate. Often people with this letter are older souls, seeking to refine themselves and share their insights with those around them.

You souls who have names that start with 'S' are the tender, over sensitive souls who are easily hurt. You are the ones who keep asking, "Why can't everyone just get along?" There is much joy in this soul and often you come across with childlike qualities. You have a marvelous ability to be able to learn anything once you put your mind to it. Your soul is a worker bee and is given much to do on earth. The challenge for you is to stay in the mental world and on your spiritual path without getting side tracked by emotions.

FIRST LETTER IS 'T'

When your soul chooses the letter 'T' with which to start the first name, it indicates a soul that can get lost in its own belief structures and finds it a challenge to go against what has been taught to you as a child. Your soul is malleable. Feed it kindness and love, and that is what your soul imitates; feeding it darkness causes your soul to then feed on the darkness. This gives a new meaning to the saying, "You are what you eat." Do you wish to be full of light or full of darkness?

Your soul is motivated to do well because it carries with it much past knowledge. The challenge for you is to use your lust for learning in the positive directions versus the negative as you are a force to be acknowledged. You need to be the very best at what you do. This is why you so often do not wish to even start an endeavor unless you feel you can master that endeavor. It is an all or nothing attitude. Your challenge is to be willing to try new things that appear difficult or outside of your range of talents. Who knows what you can truly master when you simply give it time and attention?

Your soul needs to be on top, or the bottom of the pile, for it wishes to stand out and not be somewhere caught in the middle. If you are going to do something, you'll go all out, but if you don't think you will make it to the very top, you won't even start. That is why people who's name start with the letter 'T' are at the top of their game. Your challenge is to stay in the game until you do reach the top and to give things a chance that initially don't look too appealing.

FIRST LETTER IS 'U'

Your 'U' soul seeks to understand. Your soul seeks some type of explanation for the situations in which you find yourself. It is irrelevant if the explanation makes sense or is true or false. What is important is that some type of understanding has occurred. A challenge is not to make up a somewhat plausible explanation just so you can move forward without really having to digest what was just experienced. Instead challenge yourself to delve into the depths of who you are and to seek a more definitive reason. What was the golden opportunity that your soul wished to learn from the experience? How can you apply this new knowledge in your life?

A temptation is to look at others thinking they are at fault without exploring how you have contributed to the situation. Be careful of holding yourself above the fray without taking at least a bit of the responsibility for creating the experience. Your soul is gifted with understandings beyond its years and is constantly seeking to build on this knowledge by experiencing an ever increasing venue of diverse experiences. Please acknowledge that whatever experiences are the hardest for you are actually the most valuable for it is in coming to peace with these experiences that you will do your greatest growing. Can your personality come to appreciate the gifts that your soul is creating through these experiences? You have a soul who crosses its fingers hoping that action on your part will take the jinx out of current events.

Your greatest challenge is to stay absolutely honest about everything for your honesty grows you closer to Creation and any slight dishonest holds you back from achieving your spiritual goals. This can be difficult when you love to laugh and have such a vivid imagination. Exaggeration is easy, and it does produce laughs in the people around you; yet, it is a form of dishonesty and hence counterproductive. Use your creativity to create humor instead.

FIRST LETTER IS 'V'

You 'V' souls are humble and charismatic and come into the material world with a huge challenge: not to become greedy. It is easy to see what others have and wish to have the same. It is perfectly acceptable to see what others have and then desire to also have that for yourself. The challenge is in how you perceive getting what others have for yourself. Do you involve others or do it by yourself? Your natural charismatic nature causes others to want to be with you. Can you devise a methodology whereby you help others to benefit while you are also benefitting? In other words, your challenge is to be able to create win-win situations or not to make the deal. Being fair with your fellow man is what pushes you forward. Be aware that your soul always receives what is sent out, and it doesn't have to wait long before receiving the rebound of whatever was sent.

You have an honest soul who only knows how to express its own truth. The challenge is not to come across as sounding arrogant when simply sharing what you have come to know. There is a lilt around you as your soul progresses while striving to acquire humility. It's hard to be humble when you come in with so many talents in different areas. Finding your particular gift that makes you happy is a challenge as you are so capable in so many different areas. Hint: your soul is happiest when engaged in some sort of art. Art can be expressed through cutting hair, painting, designing architectural buildings, or in a variety of different ways. The goal is not to limit self, instead to give self permission to explore what the world has to offer in its fullest. Your challenge is: how do you do it all?

FIRST LETTER IS 'W'

You have come to this earth with a large capacity to really live life. You learn from experiences, as you don't like to make the same mistake twice. Sometimes you jump into the pool before seeing if there is water in the pool. You are so ready for adventure that you occasionally fail to examine the consequences of your choices. Your challenge, and what you came to learn, is how to proceed with caution and how to have patience while maintaining your ability to think for yourself.

All things come to those who wait for results while staying active in their seeking. Go after that which pulls you while simultaneously allowing divine timing to take place. You are not to be afraid of seeking the truth, as much as you hate to make the same mistake twice. For in acknowledging that which you know, and not that which you wish were true, is the way to freedom for yourself. Reaching out to others with your adventurous, wise spirit shares your love of freedom and enables you and others who interact with you to grow in consciousness.

You have a strong soul that can accomplish all it sets out to do as long as stubbornness, anger and tendency to be a bully is kept in check. Your soul wants to be heard and is quite persuasive. Your soul knows stories and can be humorous, easily holding others' attention. Your challenge is to learn patience, how to avoid revengeful thoughts, and how to use your natural psychic abilities.

FIRST LETTER IS 'X'

You came with healing gifts, and yet, you want everything now instead of letting it take its natural course in time. Remember your natural gifts are waiting to be used, and it is naturally a slow and careful process developing those gifts. Your soul does not wish for you to rush your gifts into fruition, as then, disappointment and frustration is the result as confusion sets inside of you. Remember all things occur in perfect timing for when you are ready to properly use your gifts. Challenge yourself to examine your gifts as your soul does not wish for talents to go unexplored. Go in the direction you are led by your inner guidance system without having expectations for the results.

Allow yourself to heal past wounds, and thus, you will be able to create the space for others to heal. You do this through your great ability to carry and show love coupled with your compassion for others. Your natural talents are not to be used just for your benefit but for the good of humankind. Your challenge is not to adopt the mindset of my way or the highway, instead use your talents to heal those around you by sharing your ability to have compassion. You are here to learn to have faith. Remember, your gifts will develop, as you are ready to handle them.

The other major challenge that you face is that of tunnel vision. You get your mind set on one methodology that works for you and there you stay. Persistence is important, yet so is flexibility. A challenge in the 'X' is to stay flexible and not eliminate from your life all things that initially appear disagreeable to you. Give them time prior to saying whether something is appropriate or inappropriate for you.

FIRST LETTER IS 'Y'

Souls that choose to start a name with the letter 'Y' start out in life with challenges as they are constantly questioning the validity of spirituality and simultaneously wanting to know more. If this is your first letter, know that you are stronger than you think and know more than you think. Your gut gives you accurate data. You came to learn how to help others question long held beliefs while continually seeking new spiritual adventures yourself. The challenge for the 'Y' is not to become entangled in the material world to such an extent that they forget they are more connected to the spiritual world than here.

You are smart when you remember you are. You came to be a gift to others and to help them. However, it is you that really requires others' help as you have a difficult time commanding your world and thus get caught up in trying to command other people's worlds, instead of simply assisting them. This causes your soul to feel troubled. You are the natural leader, yet must use the leader's position wisely. Your soul seeks to be happy with your choices, so the challenge is to continue to grow and to be willing to allow others to take the lead at times.

You are encouraged to help your soul grow and assist in helping those you love also serve their purpose. Remember, the definition of courage is to be able to stand up to danger, against the odds, without flinching, showing bravery.

Your soul understands that it is one with the universe, and thus, you must keep connecting with people to stay content because you understand that it is everybody together that constitutes the whole. You are here to grow spiritually, building upon your wealth of experiential knowledge. Your challenge is how do you share your information without sounding like a totalitarian authority figure? How do you live your understandings without consistently finding fault in situations and people around you? How can you use your humor to help both you and others manage uncomfortable situations? You have a lot on your plate. Life will not always be easy for you as much is expected of you because you hold an abundance of knowledge and are expected to use it.

FIRST LETTER IS 'Z'

You came to live in the moment. Your love of life can mesmerize others and cause you to have an abundance of both positive and negative experiences. You may have a tendency not to listen to those around you for fear they are attempting to squash your experiences with life. So your challenge is to listen to others and to apply their wisdom in your world.

You are encouraged to remember that whatever your past has been, it is your past and holds great teachings for you there. Your challenge is to use your past as a learning tool and not just to plunge forward without proper reflection causing you repeat the same learning opportunity that you have already experienced.

At any time you can come to the realization and understanding of great light; in that moment, you are healed from needing to wander always seeking to find the light that you so crave. Remember, moments are precious and of most importance. Let the past stay in the past, yet remembering its lessons. Let the future take care of itself, so that you can stay focused in the present.

You often close your ears to what others are saying as you prefer to experience everything for yourself. So, your greatest challenge is to be willing to listen to the wisdom that is shared with you so that you can truly live for the relevance of the moment.

CHAPTER 4: LAST LETTER IN FIRST NAME

"Always use the proper name for things. Fear of a name increases fear of the thing itself."
J.K. Rowling

LAST LETTER IS 'A'

Your soul has realized that it is important to be liked by others, for you came here to learn how to play nicely with others. Thus, you decided which traits are agreeable and which ones are not. You have made yourself into a person who is highly likable but will not change who you are to get liked. It is important to realize that what you consider admirable traits are not necessarily what others consider to be endearing traits. Plus, similar traits can be exhibited quite differently, some more pleasantly than others.

You have come to connect with others to demonstrate that you can be an agreeable person and to get along with most people. Yet, it is not necessary to even worry about getting along with everyone. You have come to learn that just because you find certain traits appealing, it does not mean that everyone else feels the same way and to make that okay. It is important to stay true to you. Your soul wishes for you to accept you for who you are and be okay with you as you are. "Judgement is mine saith the Lord" so how about not judging yourself?

LAST LETTERS ARE 'AH'

You are one of the rare people who are truly here on a mission and have been favored or blessed by Creation. In the Bible Abram and Sarai have their names changed to Abraham and Sarah once they start their mission. Notice that 'AH' is now in both of their names and was not previously present in either name. The 'AH' at the end of a name shows favoritism and that you are here to assist others, besides increasing your own knowledge. You are a rock, steady, solid and a blessing to those around you.

When you have this combination in your name you have come to help others by leading the way to truth and living your soul's perspective. It is not for you to stay silent or to not share because you think so differently than the crowd. It is for you to guide the group in an appropriate direction versus having mob hysteria rule the day. However, it is not to demand that anyone else follows you. Your soul would like you to learn how to listen within and then to have the courage to follow what you know to be your truth.

As a side note, when the 'AH' falls in the middle of the name, like in the name Abraham, you are here on mission, the same as when its the ending of your name, but you may not accomplish your entire mission or may get sidetracked in route. An example of this is Abraham not waiting until his wife got pregnant, instead, being influenced by his wife, took matters into his own hands and had a child with his concubine Hagar.

LAST LETTER IS 'B'

You came to compete and to see if you really can be as good as you think you are. You came to raise the stakes and demand more of yourself so that you can truly embody the United State's Army slogan of, "Be the best you can be". Occasionally you decide that winning is more important that being a team player, and it is alright to do whatever is necessary to come out on top in order to be the winner. Your tenacity is impressive when you go after a goal. Yet your need to be recognized as the best can create problems for you. It can cause you to create a problem, which you then solve, so that others see you as a dynamic leader instead of you not creating the unnecessary problem in the first place.

As much as the drive to compete is innate to you, it is important to realize that choosing your battles is equally important. Your soul has asked you to come share the competitive spirit that causes everyone to want to improve, and yet your soul also wants you to learn that one does not always need to compete as your drive for competition can break up your relationships. Your soul wishes for you to learn when it is more important for you to support other people or when it is more important to compete with them. The most important truth your soul wishes for you to learn is how to appreciate yourself, so that you no longer need or crave recognition from others.

LAST LETTER IS 'C'

The 'C' in the last letter position indicates a balance between feminine and masculine traits. Occasionally this is expressed sexually; being bisexual, transexual or homosexual. More often, this balance is expressed artistically in such fields as architecture or other types of construction like airplanes or designing clothes, or even in the systematic approach to creating a new, non-symmetrical hair style. Your soul wishes for you to learn how to stay in balance without flaunting or imposing your need for balance on others. Your soul has asked you to demonstrate for others what androgyny looks like.

Your soul is happy when you have a strong support system with your family and friends. So, it is imperative that you keep your support system intact. However, because other people's support is so vital to your own contentment, it causes you to hold onto people, and occasionally things, longer than what is of value or what serves you. You are here to learn when to hold onto something or someone and when it is appropriate to let go. You are here to share your creative skills.

LAST LETTERS ARE 'CK'

Fortunate are those whose name ends with 'CK' as you have the ability to think quickly on your feet and say just the right thing. You are able to create clever comments that humor others while still making your point. The best part of this combination is that you use your quick wit to create good wages in whatever field captures your fancy as long as you do not become arrogant in your thinking. Arrogance occurs when you think you are so much smarter than others around you, and therefore, somehow better than others. Said another way, your challenge is not to let this quick thinking ability cause you to become obnoxious.

You can go in any direction and are best when not limiting yourself to one area of interest. Your challenge is to consistently use tack while keeping your wit sharp. You are here to share your smart humor, as it allows others to hear, and thus consider, a different viewpoint from their own.

LAST LETTER IS 'D'

Everybody can win when all are cooperative. Whereas, when people are competitive, it appears that someone has to lose for another to win. Your soul wishes for you to have enough experiences that will help you to decide that cooperation is more desirable than competition as win-win situations are preferred. So, your soul wishes for you to constantly strive to make things better for both yourself and others.

Your challenge is to stay cooperative when others around you create highly competitive situations, especially when your urge is to do whatever is necessary for you to get ahead. Remember that the turtle beat the hare in the most famous race of all. Your soul is happiest when you can keep the whole in mind versus self-preservation.

LAST LETTER IS 'E'

You have been gifted with a generosity of spirit. You delight in helping others accomplish their tasks, thereby feeling useful and appreciated. Others clearly see how generous you are with your time and thus can take advantage of your innate willingness to be of service. This creates a challenge for you in the area of time management. Do you assist someone else when they ask for your help, or do you complete what is on your list first? Your challenge is how to solve this never ending challenge: when do you help another and when do you decline so that your own work gets done in a timely manner without you having to extend your work day?

A suggestion for handling this dilemma is to mention that you'd be glad to help once you finish your current task. Then wait for their response. If the other person says great and walks off, then you know the other person was seeking for someone else to do their work, and anyone would do. However, if the response is asking what they can do for you to help you in your task, then you know that the other person needs your skills specifically and not just anyone would do. When this is the case it is best to state that your task won't take you long to get to a stopping point and then leave to help the other after a half hour. Why wait and not go immediately? Two reasons: you gain respect this way as you are stating your work is equally as important as theirs, and are more appreciated when you do show up.

LAST LETTERS ARE 'EY'

You have a need to rescue others as that makes you the 'good' guy. People who need to rescue also have the need to feel better about themselves. So, your soul has given you a double challenge. First to see and address why you need to rescue others. What do you get out of rescuing? Secondly, how can you support the person without rescuing the person?

Your soul wishes you to understand that when you rescue another you are giving the message that that person is not as good or as competent as you are. Being a lesser individual they need rescuing as they cannot do this for self. Thus, when you rescue you are also sending the message that you are better than the person you are rescuing. There is a karmic consequence for sending this type of message to another.

Your soul is asking you to figure out how to help another without giving the subtle message that you have more worth than they do. Can you give suggestions? Can you be happy with believing in the person when they are having a hard time believing in self? Can you be content with supporting this person and not solving the problem yourself?

LAST LETTER IS 'F'

You have discovered that it is important to be prepared for whatever could possibly happen next. Your thinking is that it is beneficial to have the right materials on hand in order to accomplish this whereas it is not necessary to run to the store for supplies first. This thinking leads to what others would consider hoarding, even though to you it is simply being prepared and ready.

Your challenge is to stay prepared without

becoming a hoarder by owning every scrap of everything that was once owned or a ridiculous number of multiples of the same thing. How many hammers are really necessary? What supplies have you had for more than twenty years and have yet to use? Could something have multiple uses instead of needing separate items for singular tasks?

Ultimately, your soul would like for you to trust that you will be okay without needing to hoard unnecessarily for the future. It is good to be prepared, and yet, it is important to also trust in the divine. If you are feeling the need to prepare, then prepare, but do it within reason. How many hammers do you actually need? Use that type of thinking to assist you in deciding what is necessary and what is extreme.

LAST LETTER IS 'G'

There is a Chinese saying that informs us that the only constant thing in our lives is change. In other words, nothing is constant as everything is always in flex. You are here to help others deal with the scary changes that occur in life, as your innate ability to be flexible causes you to be uniquely able to handle change well. Whereas most others prefer to leave things as they are; you seek out alternatives. Why not try something new and different? Your dogged determination usually serves you well.

Your soul has given yourself a hearty challenge for you to realize that the heavier the challenge the more you actually accomplish when finished, and yet you balk at having to adapt too quickly to a new situation. Your tendency is to cringe when forced to change versus when you volunteer to change. When you volunteer to change, showing others how it is done, you are changing at your pace. You are setting the speed.

However, you rebel internally when you feel forced to adapt quicker than what is comfortable for you. This appears as self-sabotaging behaviors and/or as excessive behaviors in the form of addictions. Do you drink too much? Do you rely on medications or drugs to help you through the day? Are you a shopaholic? How does your addiction present itself?

Rare is the person whose name ends in 'G' that manages to avoid having an unhealthy, highly addictive behavior pattern sometime in their life. Your soul wishes for you to realize that addictions are your replacement for not knowing how to love yourself. Your challenge is recognize your addictions when they start , and immediately question where you are not loving yourself. The most loving act is then to squash the addictions as quickly as possible. This is done by thanking your addictions for bringing your lack of self-love to your attention and then determine why you stopped loving you. What happened? Did someone say something and you believed them? Why did you choose to take their statement over your own self-love? It helps when you leave yourself the maximum amount of flexible options at all times, loving yourself, so that your habits never morph into addictions.

LAST LETTER IS 'H'

Your soul realizes that you have dharma coming your way. You have good intentions and wish well for others, just as you do for yourself. You find others easy to love, and occasionally easier to love than yourself. Your soul desires for you to go with the flow as much as possible as it does not like conflict in any form. Harmony is your motto. Your soul wishes for you to learn how to be okay with conflict; how to stand your ground, and how not to carry outer conflict inside of you. Thus, your soul's purpose is for you to go with the flow, when you can but be able to stand up for self when necessary.

Due to dharma coming your way, your soul has said that it is alright to take a break and not work any harder than you need to do. Lucky are the people whose name ends with a 'H'.

LAST LETTER IS 'I'

Your soul wants you to be able to handle

attention graciously. Do you crave more attention than what you are receiving? Does it embarrass you to get attention from others? Do you extend a story in order to receive more attention? Are your actions indicative of someone who has been deprived of attention? The soul's great desire is to learn how to accept another's attention graciously, and how to give authentic attention to others without thinking of any personal gains as a motivating factor.

LAST LETTER IS 'J'

When you have the last letter of 'J' in your name it means that you are a natural joker who relishes getting the last laugh. You can easily make fun of others but have a more difficult time when others reciprocate and make fun of you as its easy to have your feelings hurt.

Your soul wishes for you to continuing bringing humor to others and at the same time be able to laugh at yourself. It is also important not to use humor that is at someone else's expense. The challenge is not to go into subtle put-down humor, or to make fun of another thinking its okay as long as its done with humor.

Good, clean, intelligent humor is what is desired for you to master. You are smart enough to master this trait. The question is, are you willing to do so?

LAST LETTER IS 'K'

Your soul has blessed you having a 'K' for the last letter in your name as that indicates that you will always be able to make a good living. The challenge for you is to not become screwed in order to make your dreams come true. It is also important for you to keep in mind that money is only one form of wealth and that true wealth is inner peace.

Your challenge is to create a good income while remembering what is really important in life. Stay focused on what what really counts, those things that are eternal in nature and not temporary like material goods.

LAST LETTER IS 'L'

Your soul sees the value in who you are and what you have to contribute. The question is, do you? As you age you will gain in self-confidence and every year will get better than the previous year. Your soul wishes for you to become self assured as you age, so that as you gain in confidence, you don't become conceited at the same time.

Your challenge is to stay compassionate while you gain in your knowledge of who you really are and why you are here. As you gain in self-assurance, can you simultaneously assist others in also gaining in their perspective of self?

LAST LETTER IS 'N'

There are multiple gifts and challenges that come with having 'N' as the last letter in your name. Your soul has gifted you with an incredible memory so that you can use that memory to help others stay authentic and grounded. However, the challenge in having good memory is not to belittle those that don't. The other challenge is not to get so tied up in the minutia that you drive others crazy with too many details. How do you know when to stop sharing?

The second challenge in having 'N' as your last letter is your obsession with survival. That is because you are a realist and wish to see things as they are, not as you wish them to be. It is difficult not to obsess over survival because you can see things realistically. The goal is to become at peace with the knowledge that you will survive as long as you are meant to survive, as written in your contract with God.

LAST LETTERS ARE 'NN'

Your memory has been enhanced as well as your ability to bore others with minutia. People with a double 'N' are often accused of having a photographic memory. Your gift is having a remarkable memory in the area of your choice. Your soul wishes for you to use this to your advantage and the advantage of others.

The challenge is to not belittle unimportant details when with others. Everyone doesn't have this remarkable memory, and may not remember the details as accurately as yourself. When the details are not that important, it is important to let things ride and not correct others. Be gracious that you were blessed with a fabulous memory, and use your remarkable memory to assist others to learn instead of having impatient with others as their memories are not as gifted as yours.

LAST LETTER IS 'O'

Just like Marco Polo, you wish to be remembered for what you have accomplished and how you have treated others. You will be remembered, so decide whether you wish to be remembered for something positive or something negative.

Another gift and accompanying challenge with the 'O' is the need and desire for plain old fashion fun. It is delightful to be able to remind people how to have fun and to encourage fun. It is another thing though to promote fun when there is work to be done; or to take fun to the extreme and it ends up costing someone. The goal is to have fun, and to limit fun when not appropriate; to keep your delightful playfulness and yet be serious when necessary.

LAST LETTER IS 'P'

The 'P' remains the same regardless if it is in the middle of the name or the last letter in the name. Read what 'P' means in the middle of a name.

LAST LETTER IS 'Q'

The soul of the person with the last letter of 'Q' is recognizing that they don't fit in with the pack. They follow their own drum. This soul has its own path and wishes to be considered unique and special. Herein lies the challenge: how do you play your own song, on your own drum, when you are part of an orchestra?

How do you play your song, knowing you are different and unique without causing others to feel you think you are better than them, or 'special'? How do you play your song, loudly and clearly, without alienating others? Your gift is your song. Your challenge is how to share it without offending others. May your soul find your path so that others learn your tune with you.

LAST LETTER IS 'R'

Your soul is inquisitive and wishes to experience as much as possible. Your soul wishes nothing other than the truth and to experience things for itself. Your soul will know the truth for that which registers in your soul is truth. Your soul is rebellious, and has a hard time following directions, especially ones that don't agree with you.

Your soul wishes to experience the multiplicity

of possible experiences and to learn from each one. Your soul's desire is for you to grow into your own understanding of each experience so that you own the experience. You have much knowledge, but knowledge not experienced is not valued.

Your soul is adventurous. You are here to have adventures and learn from them while also learning how to negotiate fairly when given directions that are illogical to you.

LAST LETTERS ARE 'RK'

You have mighty ambitions. Your soul pushes hard for you to go forward and do well. Your challenge is to land on target for your goals without missing the mark multiple times first.

LAST LETTER IS 'S'

Your soul loves to learn and wants to

capitalize on it's ability to continually learn. Since you are constantly learning something new you may over evaluate your decisions. You naturally pay attention to numerous details.

Your soul wants you to learn to trust your own decisions; to know that you made the best decision that you could with the knowledge that you currently have. Your soul is excited to go forward and does not go in reverse well.

Your challenge is to go forward without looking backwards. Yes, reflect, but let your past be your past. Take the knowledge that you have accrued and use it to go forward in the direction of your choice. Your soul is happy when it is progressing.

LAST LETTER IS 'T'

Your soul is a dynamite soul and wants to progress as rapidly as possible. You can be incredibly considerate. The challenge is to be just as considerate when not getting your own way as you are when getting what you desire.

You can be a bulldozer, who takes things to the extreme in responsibility, in your physical activities and/or whatever activity pleases you the most. Your soul wishes for you to learn moderation and to continue to be responsible even when you don't wish to be so.

LAST LETTER IS 'U'

Your personality wishes to be unique in some way, so you do things in order to get attention. You have so many gifts, and yet you deny yourself the simple pleasures in life until you miss them so much you overindulge. Your soul wants you to find balance enjoying life while also realizing that another's attention isn't really what you desire. Instead your true desire is to connect with the divine.

You may have difficulty at times recalling what it is that makes you happy. So, when happy, you want to over indulge in order to prolong the moment. Your soul asks that you cherish the happy moments and allow yourself to throughly enjoy them, however long they last. For those are the moments you are actually the closest to the divine.

LAST LETTERS ARE 'UA'

The amazing combination of the letters 'U' and 'A' together indicates that you possess knowledge beyond ones' chronological years. It often indicates that you are two years ahead academically as well as two years behind emotionally. Not to worry as you will eventually catch up with yourself around the age of twenty-eight.

Your soul is an old soul who is so far ahead of the pack that you often feel you are behind as you know you don't fit in somehow. Thus you may indulge in activities, like drinking, to subconsciously lower your vibration in order to fit in with crowd. Your challenge is to be you, realize that your differences are what makes you so special, and that others will eventually want to be more like you. Thus, there is no need to attempt to fit in with others since they will eventually change to want to fit in with you.

LAST LETTER IS 'V'

You are charming, charismatic and have sex appeal, just as much as Gustav did in "Beauty and the Beast". With so much going for you, you can occasionally become arrogant and entitled.

Your soul wishes for you to understand that sexual energy and spiritual energy is the same. What is important and what matters is how you direct that energy and use it. Your goal is to stay in balance and use your energy with intention and not to satisfy lustful thoughts.

LAST LETTER IS 'W'

You have perfected the fight or flight syndrome when feeling uncomfortable. Your soul wants you to learn how to feel comfortable regardless of where you are, and with whom. Your soul mentally understands that all of humanity is one, yet individually has problems dealing with situations where everyone certainly doesn't feel like they are one with each other.

Your challenge is to feel like everyone is important and a part of the whole while you grasp with being human and wanting to judge. Your soul wishes for you to learn how to feel comfortable with yourself, so that you can feel comfortable with everyone else and wherever you are.

LAST LETTER IS 'X'

You have an inquisitive mind, one that wants to find out things for yourself. You don't appreciate others telling you the answers for you do wish to discover the answers for yourself. You want to make things better for others for whom you care. Your soul is strong and persistent.

Your challenge is to find your own answers while not getting upset with those who love you and wish to share their knowledge with you. They are not thinking that they are robbing you of the quest, but that they are providing a shortcut and trying to be of assistance. When you shift your attitude, you will find that your soul and your personality align beautifully to provide for you what it is that you truly want.

LAST LETTER IS 'Y'

You are a chameleon and can get along with anyone you wish to get along. However, the need to get along and please others overrides you being who you really are at all times. Your soul wishes for you to be able to get along with others while simultaneously not altering who you are in order to please others. Your soul wants you to make decisions based on who you are, and how you would like to be perceived to be, and not made on whom you wish to please.

LAST LETTER IS 'Z'

You gave yourself a large challenge to overcome as you do not like to listen to others. Others would consider that you have a close mind because they do not understand that you really are here to find out everything on your own. You don't mean to dismiss what you are told, you simply think others don't know really know what they are doing.

Your soul wants you to take an easier route by at least listening to others prior to dismissing their thoughts. Your challenge is to know when to accept another's suggestions and when to trust yourself to do things your own way. You have a tough road to follow as your soul is so independent and stubborn that you often make things harder than they need to be.

CHAPTER 5:
MIDDLE LETTER IN FIRST NAME

"It ain't what they call you, it's what you answer to." W.C. Fields

Our soul purpose on earth is to develop our consciousness. A side benefit to a higher consciousness is the ability to feel and express unconditional love. The middle letters in your name indicate the harder areas where improvement/growth is wanted. We are called to have both a mind and a heart, as integrating emotions with the mind is the solution to unity, which creates a higher level of consciousness. Hatred is only possible in this matrix and not outside of it, as duality is here. Mistrust is built into the matrix. Instead, it is important to realize it is safe to feel or to think outside of the norm.

The matrix was built on dependency, following rules, and limited emotional responses. So mastering ones' emotions, and using our minds to help us master our emotions, is the way out of the matrix. Remember we chose to come into the matrix where things are distorted in order to change the blueprint. The Matrix encourages a lower frequency, while Creation encourages a higher vibration. The Matrix distorts true spirituality. Our names help to remind us of the uncontaminated spirit that we are.

The middle letters show where our greatest challenges are, the ones we are most scared to own, and thus are the most difficult to conquer. We connect with spirit by claiming our challenges and taking responsibility for them. We are encouraged to master our emotions and eliminate our addictions, such as fear, sex, alcohol, drugs, and blaming others for our choices. That does not mean to not indulge; it does mean that we are the ones that stay in control instead of having our addictions control us. This is done by keeping all things in balance. For example, enjoy a glass or two of wine, but stop there so not to overindulge and be out of balance. [20]

Another challenge is when our masculine self fights our feminine self, which is another way to keep us in the matrix. This is also expressed externally with males fighting each other and/or degrading females or vice-versa, thus keeping the masses enslaved and our societies in the matrix. That is why it is so important to honor both sexes so that we, in oneness, can depart this Matrix.

We are encouraged to use our pure imagination to create pure thought, uncontaminated by negativity. Thought causes creation to manifest. Reflection and altering our thoughts and actions releases the challenges indicated in our letters, and allows us to use our gifts more freely.

---

20 one of the signs of alcoholism is needing four or more glasses of an alcoholic beverage in one sitting

MIDDLE LETTER IS 'A'

You are a person who literally hates to be told what to do; instead you want to be asked. When asked you are pretty compliant, but when told, your rebellious streak is activated. You also don't like to do any more work than is necessary as you know that a balance between work and play is important.

Your soul finds it challenging to follow directions that have little to no merit, which is why you learned early to despise others telling you what to do. Your soul is hoping to learn how to say no politely and also how not to go off center when pushed to do something that your will does not want to do. How do you develop and use mediation skills to speak your mind and not insult the ones around you at the same time? How do you phrase things so that no one feels badly at the end of the conversation and you don't get stuck doing more work than you wish to do? The main lesson of this letter is to learn self-control so that no one else can push your buttons by simply telling you what to do.

You were born with an excellent mind, one

capable of much learning, one that constantly is eager to learn and put disparate pieces of information together so that it makes sense. Your soul is eager to grow; to learn how the world really works and how the universe works. Your soul wants to find how it fits into the whole scheme of things and what exactly that scheme is. Your soul wants to know that it matters.

In order to learn this valuable piece of information, you have been gifted with being agile, artistic, coordinated and you are no one's fool. Put the pieces together. Learn as much as you can while also leaving time to play.

Remember that there is no time to be negative, or to doubt. Your soul is strong and wants to move forward. Anything that falls on the negative spectrum is a distraction and slows you down. When you stay around positive people it is easier to stay positive. Stay connected to your soul, remember it, and all will go well.

MIDDLE LETTER IS 'B'

Your soul wishes to have proof of every thing, so you tend to study, to research, and to do your best. You have a tendency to be supercritical and are not afraid of expressing what you think. Thus your words can be like acid when being received by others.

Your personality finds it hard to believe in hidden knowledge, things that are not written as you like proof. You are very intuitive, which causes problems as you don't want to believe in things that are not written or can be proven. You are very moral but can be close minded and be unwilling to change your opinions.

Your challenge is to stop kicking yourself for being impulsive, instead work to stop yourself from acting on your impulses until you've had a chance to consider consequences of your proposed action. Because you do not want others to realize how impulsive you really are, you can become clandestine, sneaky and duplicitous.

Your goal is to reign in your impulses and to quench your thirst for other's approval and to take from others without asking first. Your soul does best when nourished by others. So, realize you crave affection, and use your talents to build things up and not to tear things down.

MIDDLE LETTER IS 'C'

Your soul contains a high spiritual force but you can deny that force, or you can refuse to believe the force even exists. This universal force, that runs in your veins, is to be used for the highest good of everyone around you. You know right from wrong, but do you wish to use your force for good or for power? Your challenge is not to get tempted to acquire the material aspects of life as then you would become insensitive to others and misuse your numerous gifts. You will then be following your lower instincts. As the saying goes, "To those whom much is given, much is expected." However, do not over commit yourself as that results in self-destruction.

Your business acumen is strong. You have the ability to use mental telepathy, but you may just call it hunches. You do your best in business when it is a partnership. Just as you do your best when married. It is important to believe in yourself.

Your soul wants you to bring spirituality to others, to use your natural creative abilities and to think for yourself. You may be tempted to use sex as a weapon to destroy, you can be lustful because you have high ambitions. Above all else, your soul wants you to be aware of your actions on others. Do not take out your frustrations when your ambitions are not met on the road to a false security.

Your challenge is to avoid rivalry, as that is the ruin of you and the ones you love. Careful of becoming selfish, and not being concerned with the welfare of others. You are so powerful that any destructive thought against another will boomerang; so don't give into ugly thoughts. Maintain an atmosphere of love and constructive efforts in order to succeed.

MIDDLE LETTER IS 'D'

Your soul is highly disciplined, so much so that others may consider you boring. However, you have the visualization process down, and are able to realize your dreams. Your personality is unduly afraid when financially or emotionally unstable, and will tend to fight all forms of discipline. Your challenge is to go with your soul's strengths and not to fight them.

Your soul flourishes with it's divine connection as you naturally absorb the electromagnetic excesses that healers carry. Said another way, you have natural healing abilities if you chose to develop them. Your energy is recharged when in nature, thus nature is critical to your soul. Nature is your elixir.

You may cling to religion due to your innate healing abilities giving the Unknown your gratitude. However, you are not meant to stay in a religious state of mind. Instead, your soul asks that you raise your vibration and become more spiritual. The difference for you is accepting what is taught to you in religion and using those principles to make your own decisions.

Your challenge this lifetime is to change ignorant ideas into knowledge, to take limitations, especially those self-imposed, and change them into opportunities. It is easy for you to become depressed or despondent and your soul wants you to change those feelings into strong convictions. Your soul knows that you believe work comes first and that your need for security is strong, however, your soul wishes for you to expand your interests beyond work as to avoid becoming dull and boring, and to take your love of family and become more comfortable showing your family how much you love them versus just telling them.

MIDDLE LETTER IS 'E'

You treasure law, religion, written or unwritten trends of nature, and are receptive to the divine force. You listen well to others and you are talented at hearing both what they say and what they do not say. As such, you give good advice.

Your soul's challenge is to move these energies in through the body and to own them and not to be afraid of feelings and the compassionate vibrations that you receive from others. The next goal is to stay positive and not be critical of others nor forget to be tactful as sometimes you forget to use your filtering devise and can be quite negative.

You have such a strong will, are usually extroverted and wonderful communicators. In order to be at your best you require a good education, and to know how to tame your restlessness. Your soul wishes for you to use your free will intelligently, to tame your restless nature, to use tact when using your strong communication skills and to continue to help others with your skills.

Your soul loves to laugh, play and simply have fun. How can you honor your gifts without resorting to the negative side of lying, exaggerating and needing to pull others into sob stories to give you more attention? You have quite a gift with this letter. Are you up to your challenges and what your soul wishes for you to learn?

MIDDLE LETTER IS 'F'

Your soul wants you to be able to discover the mysteries of the universe by studying the different religions, and by living your faith. This is important to your soul as you have enjoyed living in illusion more than reality. Your soul wishes for you to progress in this lifetime by being willing to see that which is really there and not just that which you wish to see.

In the past you have used trickery, cleverness and untruths to slant the truth to your favor. Thus, you have shadow energy that your soul wishes to shed this time around. You redeem yourself by motivating yourself and others to action that is beneficial to all involved. Consider yourself the caterpillar who gets to become the butterfly.

Your soul wants you to release your doubts back into the universe, to become more self-assertive as you become more self-assured and to be willing to see the truth thus freeing yourself from illusion. Your soul loves you so much that it gave you a way to monitor your progress. Watch your need to collect, keep and hoard material items to such an extant that it is way beyond what you could ever use. The less you hoard, the less you doubt, the more progress you will be making.

MIDDLE LETTER IS 'G'

Your soul wants to maximize its opportunity to be here by doing as much growth as possible while on earth. In the past you have had a hard time keeping secrets and could overindulge in food and alcohol in order to avoid fully living on the earth.

Your soul is highly sensitive and intuitive, and as such doesn't like to hear bad news. Yet, the world gives you what you interpret to be hurtful news on a regular basis, so how do you deal with all of the perceived negativity? Instead of dealing with the issue head on, you have done your best to negate it by numbing yourself through excessive food and/or alcohol. If you cave into your cravings, or wish to escape reality, it can cause you to be considered insane.

There is a high rate of insanity with this letter due to dual thinking. Save yourself from the dire consequences of not progressing this time around.

Your challenge is considerable. Your soul is asking you to stay active, to be involved with others, and to do not sit down for any extended period of time. Instead, seek enlightenment; take a risk and marry either a person or your job so that you have purpose in your life. Most important of all, minimize your excesses so that over-indulgence is not in your world.

MIDDLE LETTER IS 'H'

Your soul has worked hard and learned plenty prior to coming into this life. Therefore, you are gifted with being balanced, wanting justice for yourself and others, and what may, at times, seem like a curse, but it really is a gift, of people immediately being attracted to you or repulsed by you. You would make a good judge in the courtroom, or a good manager in a job as you represent the balance between what is right by man's law and what is right by universal law, plus you have the ability not only to listen, but to actually hear what is being said on multiple levels.

Your challenge is not to use these gifts to judge others as any thought or desire projected to another will in time return to influence you. Your goal is not to judge, instead assume an attitude of unbending justice from God or nature to protect you. Definitely, do not retaliate when wronged as retaliation attracts dangerous situations to you.

There is a fine line between guiding others as you are talented in doing and telling them what to do as if you were the great Sphinx or the Phoenix Risen. Use your intuitive gifts and connection to spirit to guide and make suggestions only. Your soul asks that you learn this distinction and use it appropriately.

You can monitor how well you are doing by monitoring your thoughts to see if they go towards revenge and getting even, or if you prefer luxury and worship money. That is the negative side, while the positive is when you are involved in earthly endeavors helping others.

Your soul wants to be used as a positive force in this world; yet one that doesn't use force to accomplish tasks.

MIDDLE LETTER IS 'I'

Your soul is an independent soul who wants to do things your own way. One who will take input from others, but stubbornly holds on to its own ideals. Your soul longs to fit in with others and simultaneously does not want to fit in with others as it wishes to stand out from the crowd. How do you accomplish both?

Your soul wishes to learn on its own, from its own experiences versus books and from others. What worked for one, or some, may not work for the 'I', so the 'I' needs to go find out for itself. Then, and only then, will the 'I' in the second to last position feel satisfied. Your soul wishes for you to discern when it is best to work alone and when you can benefit from learning from others. Regardless of where you collect the information that you use to make your decisions, make your final decision independently. That means you use the data collected, consider all of it including how you feel inside, and then make your decision. Don't be in a hurry, as you make better choices when you have had ample reflection and thought time.

Your goal is to remember to speak with intention but not for attention. As much as you need to be independent, you also need to be included, so include others and keep your own council. Your challenge is timing: to know when to do what. Trust your heart and release your mind from the burden of trying to figure out the timing issue. When you follow your heart, you win. When you follow your mind, you capitulate between winning and becoming so frustrated that you lose. Allow your natural leadership skills to rule the day.

MIDDLE LETTER IS 'J'

Your soul has the ability to shortcut the thinking processes by subconsciously using your unconscious mind. This translates as the ability to almost hypnotize people to hang on to every word you say. Said another way, you are intuitive, can mesmerism others, and can share electric sparks with your eyes. You think quicker than most.

Your soul came to take the road less traveled, to experience and seek uncommon pursuits, and to have unconventional relationships. In order to accomplish these tasks, you will experience the extremes in life, have money and lose it only to have it again, have loving relationships and lose them only to have loving relationships again, and to have great jobs and opportunities only to lose them before gaining new ones.

This need to forge your own path and the up and down cycle of gain and lost is there to show you how witty and clever you are and challenge you not to go into depression, lose confidence in yourself, or attempt to escape life through excessive drinking and partying. When thinking negatively, you can become dishonest, and self-destructive instead of balancing yourself so that you can advance self along the path of knowledge.

Your soul wants you to use your intelligent sense of humor coupled with your shear brilliance to dynamically live a life that others envy and wish to follow. Your soul is one that wants to demonstrate on the earth how life can be lived and to encourage others to follow their own path and not be a slave to conventional ideas and pathways.

Your goal is to use all of your myriad of talents wisely so that you can reap your reward of easily becoming a millionaire, easily managing manifesting your dreams and best of all, easily loving another. To help you accomplish this great goal, your soul encourages you to study the Jewish Tree of Life as that is where your answers lay, since no one else can answer the type of questions you have for you.

MIDDLE LETTER IS 'K'

Your soul vibrates and connects to one of the highest spiritual forces. Thus you have mental telepathy whether you acknowledge it or not.

This vibration causes you to be overly sensitive and highly intuitive. Thus, you will benefit when following your hunches. Part of your goal, like all people who carry high vibrations, is to share your understanding of spirituality with others. Notice, we did not say religion, for people can get religion on their own. How do you raise the vibration of one's religious understandings to one of spiritual understandings? That is one of your challenges.

Your soul can be a genius in your area of interest, yet you must believe in your own ability, and be just with others in order to succeed. Your soul wants you to take advantage of opportunities when they present themselves, yet not to become materialistically greedy. Again, you gain when you share by assisting others to also gain. You are like the captain of the ship, either you all arrive together or you all sink together. Your soul wants you to find a way to sail your ship successfully. To do so, you must learn to keep secrets, not to have loose lips, and not to be overly forceful.

Your soul's challenge is to find harmony within yourself and to be at peace with the divine. It is also to learn how to express love spiritually, not only physically. Your soul loves to laugh and find the humor in situations, which is why it resonates to a higher vibration. So laugh, stay creative and be who you wish to be, and not what others expect you to be.

Remember, good or bad, your fortune is dominated by your personality's will. It is fortunate indeed when the personality aligns with the soul's desires.

MIDDLE LETTER IS 'L'

Your soul has gifted your personality with good reasoning skills, a warm heart, being inspirational, sexy and with a legal mind that incorporates spiritual knowledge. You will sacrifice when necessary and have tremendous compassion towards others.

Your soul wants you to take full advantage of being in a body by learning to make good decisions so that you are no longer indecisive; to learn to forgive your enemies of which you will have more than your fair share; and not to commit suicide or self-destruct.

You will repeatedly be disappointed if you build hope on false foundations, principles, or promises. It is also prudent to allow your wonderful mind to explore all options prior to making any decisions.

You are psychic and psychic people are often overly sensitive; constantly changing their minds where it's difficult to make permanent decisions; prone to suicide; highly compassionate; can be used or walked on; and needy of praise. Fortunately they are lovable so it's hard to stay mad at sensitive people.

Your salvation is via your religious devotion, and spiritual quest, because you are one of these gifted psychics. Your main goal this lifetime is to clear up past live karmas so you are no longer tied to the past in any manner and to do whatever steps are necessary to enhance your own enlightenment. You have a tendency to hold on to people and things way past when it is beneficial to do so.

The most important thing your soul wants you to know is that you need to be ready for death at any time. You may look more youthful than your age, yet you may die quickly and unexpectedly and possibly violently. The possibility of violence is enhanced if your spiritual knowledge was used selfishly or for any purpose other than the highest good of all involved.

Due to the proclivity for an unexpected death, it is vitally important that you consciously sacrifice for the good of all; do without so that others may advance; devote your studies to progressing your understanding of the divine and use your analytical mind to be inspirational to others.

You would be advised to lead your life as if every day is your last day as indeed it may be so. Your greatest challenge will be that when it does come your time to pass, that you go with gratitude and love in your heart and be able to hold that feeling and belief while passing. You, most likely, are on your third initiation, and being able to pass suddenly with love still in your heart, is a requirement of that initiation.

MIDDLE LETTER IS 'M'

Your soul is here to transform itself, to experience emotional death multiple times and each time rise again to new beginnings like a Phoenix from the ashes. In order to rise again you are being asked to stop your overindulgence, your fascination with death and dying, daredevil or prideful activities, and any and all entitlement that you may feel or think.

Your soul endowed you with numerous gifts where you can manifest anything you continuously focus upon, including having the capability of being a fabulous chef or a kahuna. You find it easy to motivate others, that is once you believe in something, and are gifted in business endeavors. Hopefully you will spend your money on constructive measures that assist others and not on just your own guilty pleasures.[21]

You also have many challenges to overcome, negative personality characteristics such as hostility and animosity and participating in violence, either as the perpetrator or victim.

---
21 A person regarded as having access to, and influence in, the world of good and evil spirits, especially among some peoples of northern Asia and North America.

Another challenge is your tendency to drink too much whereas you can become an alcoholic, or you could overuse drugs sometime in your life. These activities often cause an early death for this most difficult lifetime.

Triumphing over these and other temptations is your most pronounced goal. In order to succeed you will first need to heal from all past hurts and injustices. In order to heal, you must remember the lesson learned from the hurt while also forgiving yourself, and others, for causing the pain. This way you can release the emotional pain whereas it does not influence your future actions.

Adapt and be triumphant. Be careful with your choice of words and you will triumph. Turn this most challenging life into one of spiritual ecstasy. You have a chance to be a David against Goliath. The rest of us are rooting for you to be successful and will assist you if you let us. You can manifest miracles when you focus on your positive aspects and eliminate your negative challenges.

MIDDLE LETTER IS 'N'

Your soul needs love in order to function well. Remember, devotion is the key to love. In order to feel the contentment of peace and love you must first master your thoughts and emotions for you are to be well grounded and remind others how to ground themselves. You do your best when in love as it helps you blend all of your worlds, the emotional, mental and spiritual worlds while the partnership also contributes to both people being more sensitive to the world of spirit. Companionship is vital to your life so much so that being celibate is not healthy for you as sex regenerates you.

Your soul is seeking knowledge, even as you are not great in school unless you also have an A in your name. Regardless, you have the potential to be a self-taught genius in the area of your choice as you have almost instantaneous absorption of new ideas. The color yellow enhances your ability to absorb ideas. Your intense drive for success is what carries you through and can cause others to consider you a workaholic. You literally embrace work and are good with details. Your goal is to plan your work and work your plans.

Your love of new ideas and highly developed intuition helps you to accomplish your soul's greatest desire, which is to learn from others until you can become your own teacher, especially in the spiritual realms.

You have come with much soul knowledge upon which to build, you have patience, perseverance, versatility and you remind us how to forgive. However, these gifts come with a warning, which is not to become stubborn, or righteous.

Be aware that you will have an unconventional life style that may encompass many moves, or lots of changes in your original arrangements and plans. You are extremely flexible so this is exciting and not problematic. Your goal is to stay connected to your spiritual understandings while simultaneously presenting new ideas to others.

MIDDLE LETTER IS 'O'

Blessed is this soul as your soul has increased spiritual awareness, psychic ability, accurate dreams, and the gift of prophesy. All that needs to be accomplished is to attune oneself to the universe. This can be done by meditation or adopting other spiritual practices.

If you reject your spiritual gifts you shall become accident prone, get divorced due to diminishing communication, get sick or have an abortion, and/or even have to deal with jail or a different type of bondage. In other words, catastrophe after catastrophe can happen if you go against your soul and against your contract with God.

Your soul's greatest challenge is to stay on path, to play out the contract that you came to live, and to utilize the gifts that you have so abundantly be given. Use your gifts wisely as they are treasures and were hard won by you prior to being born.

MIDDLE LETTER IS 'P'

Your soul is here to play and remind everyone else how to play, especially those souls that become so focused that they forget to laugh and take time out to relax. Your gift of communication morphs into being able to use your words to persuade others to change their thinking. Your challenge is to keep communicating and not to refuse to discuss topics you consider distasteful or ones that require your emotions to be vulnerable.

Your goal is to remember to be honest as lying is not only deceptive, it cuts the connection you have between your soul and your personality so that each one operates independently. This, in itself, would stop you from achieving your goals for this lifetime. So, be truthful, and remember to use tack. Keep your hope alive, and your faith strong. Be a positive influence in other's lives.

MIDDLE LETTER IS 'Q'

Your soul is here to experience polarity; happiness and unhappiness, to have children and to have them leave home so you are without children; unbridled joy and extreme depression. It's what you do to balance yourself that is important. Your challenge is to experience as much as you can without falling into a deep depression or any other negative emotion for prolonged period of times as that damages relationships.

You work better when working with a companion than you do alone as you have enough inspiration and creative energy for two people. Your goal is to maintain your inner haven and not allow anything that stems form the material world, or other people, to destroy it. as you are inspired when content.

MIDDLE LETTER IS 'R'

Your soul seeks the truth and thus has no

tolerance for liars and anything that lacks ethics. You rarely give a second chance to the person who was out of integrity.

Your life can change in an instance as you normally gain insights quickly. Your intuition is heightened by shocking news. Others will marvel at how quickly you recover from horrific news, and even worse experiences, like rape, horrible accidents and natural disasters. Tragedy causes you to use your analytical brain, coupled with your insights, to gain greater understanding of spirit which causes enlightenment.

Your challenge is to keep striving to learn more, to keep growing in your spiritual abilities, to be open to having unexplainable experiences. You could have a near death experience in order to appreciate life more. You goal is to ascend to higher vibrations so that you can ascend, possibly like Elijah, Yeshua, and Mohammad. Your goal is to attain immortality.

MIDDLE LETTER IS 'S'

You can be really, really smart and do really, really stupid things. Your soul wishes you to be successful, however you'll need to fail first to really appreciate success unless you can learn to appreciate your gifts early in life. Your challenge is to become responsible for your choices, actions and beliefs; not to blame another for anything, but instead relish in being you.

Your soul wishes for you to use your charisma, together with love and courage, to find the strength to go the distance in mastering your mind and emotions so that you can find your peace with God from within. Daily meditation, prayer, and reading inspirational material is the way you will grow.

Your challenge is to see if you can attain sainthood. Can you apply that which you know to your every day life? Can you state your truth in such a way that you consider how your actions will affect others prior to taking an action.

In order to become a saint, you must have

knowledge, compassion and be willing to take risks. You are an overachiever who must avoid getting bored where you start something and don't finish it. Avoid procrastination. Combine your good memory with your natural ambition to grow your psychic abilities so that you can combine the best of the world with the best of spirit and truly have others feel you are a saint. Your soul plans for you to accomplish the impossible in this lifetime as your soul knows that within the word 'impossible' is the word 'I'm possible.'

MIDDLE LETTER IS 'T'

You like to take everything to the extremes. What you like, you really, really like. What you don't like, you simply don't want to do. When positive you have wisdom, are protective of family and able to see the dignity in others. When feeling negative, you become selfish, tend to be materialistic and either become withdrawn or quarrelsome. Remember that all physical things eventually pass away.

It is important to note that before a soul can pass to any of the higher realms, every debt to Nature and God must be paid. Imprudence threatens to encompass you with ruin, and you will be expected to pay for your folly or foolishness, unless you immediately change your ways. Seek your soul mates, who are rarely relatives. What goes around, comes around.

All efforts expended in constructive channels increase the ability for real soul advancement while the converse is also true. Remember at the end of this world what really matters is not your material stuff and what we were able to buy, nor our level of success. What really matters is what you built, who you are and how your life contributed to the lives of others. It is your character that counts and a life lived full of love.

Your soul wants you to realize that you are uniquely tied to the physical. So, explore sports, sex, and foods through a myriad of activities. It is beneficial if you would do something athletic when you get upset, like running or swimming, to help you discharge your extra energy. Your challenge is to reign in your tendency to be a perfectionist, and learn how to overcome physical desires.

Remember, you are a spiritual being learning how to be human. Your soul wants so much. You are at your best when sharing with a partner as that brings out your positive traits.

Your challenges are to control your temper, and your impatience with people who are slower than you are. Cancel the sarcasm and stop carrying grudges. You are invited to express your emotions in a constructive manner without stuffing any of them inside hoping that by burying your emotions you'll stop feeling them.

Your goals is to be honest in your relationships and not to belittle others nor create or spread falsehoods about them. Your soul gave you quite a task expecting you to either soar brilliantly like the eagle or swim lowly like the Fangtooth fish. [22]

MIDDLE LETTER IS 'U' OR 'V'

Your soul has quite a job, as it is diametrically opposed to your personality. Your soul loves to

---

[22] The nightmarish Fangtooth is among the deepest-living fish ever discovered. The fish's normal habitat ranges as high as about 6,500 feet (2,000 meters), but it has been found swimming at icy, crushing depths near 16,500 feet (5,000 meters).

love and is in love with beauty, arts, music and luxury. Your personality is prone to addiction problems, and would rather rest, play and yield to worldly temptations than to take the soul's pathway. Your personality is drawn to weak people that you can either use or control in some manner. Your personality loves to have fun, is greedy, materialistic, gives the silent treatment to others, and can be jealous, temperamental and sarcastic. Your personality is so motivated by your desires that you could end up being a criminal while attempting to satisfy those desires.

On the other hand your soul is smart, and has the ability to heal using sound waves. Your soul is wanting you to learn to let go and allow things to be as they are. Your soul wishes you to find a positive outlet for your emotions so you don't hold them inside for too long. Your soul knows how to heal via sound, and wants you to use that knowledge and your fabulous articulation skills to assist others, instead of using your desires to minimize other people's dreams and ideas, or dampen their spirits. Your soul wants you to learn how to be selfless, and how to become consistently warm and spiritual. Your goal is to have your soul monitor your personality in such a way that you can incorporate the better aspects of your personality with your soul to have a beneficial life.

MIDDLE LETTER IS 'W'

Pythagoras [23] stressed the value of wisdom and your soul agrees. Your soul desires you to experience your knowledge so that you increase your understanding of your knowledge. You are able to feel the extremes of emotional depths and highs. Your soul whispers to you continually such that you hear subtle voices from within you.

Your soul is wise and wishes you to transcend your transgressions by accepting the God's will for you. Said another way, you are here to change your personality's willfulness into your soul's willingness.

You need freedom, are naturally sensitive,

---

[23] Pythagoras was a philosopher and mathematician, best known for his theory of a triangle, where the sum of the squares of the two legs equals the square of the hypothenuse.

and a bit over-indulgent. Your goal is to change your level of consciousness as that is your way out of the matrix. You are desperate to get off the cycle of reincarnation. In order to do that you can develop an addiction to concepts that are strange, occult, or the opposite of righteous.

The use of deprivation, misfortunes, and barriers in your life are present to make you strong, so that you live life without fear. Your goal is to overcome your need for self-preservation so that your cosmic soul can become dominant. Your challenge is not to attempt to be better than others in a bid to cover your own insecurities as it doesn't serve you.

MIDDLE LETTER IS 'X'

Your soul is tempted to go to the dark side as it finds occult knowledge and evil rituals fascinating. You are intrigued by black magic, hidden knowledge, and the trials and tribulations of others. Thus your personality can be immersed in the seven deadly sins:

avarice, envy, wrath, sloth, gluttony, lust; and pride. [24]

When you choose the Light you can feel mother earth's pains, which allows you to sense natural disasters, like earthquakes, before they happen. Your soul wants to guide your personality through the trials and tribulations of life so that your intense hatred of life does not cause you to become that which you despise. Remember, you attract to you that which you focus upon, and that which carries a strong emotion. Hatred indeed is one of the strongest emotions.

Your challenge is to override your negative interests, and your fascination with witchcraft and other black magic arts . Instead replace these urges focusing on the light and how you can assist others with patience and love versus magic and darkness. An example of someone who went in the direction you are tempted to go is Alister Crowley.[25] Instead, you are encouraged to use your skills for the Light.

Your soul overrides your personality. Yet, in this case, it is your personality's goal to override

---
[24] Wikipedia definition of seven deadly sins.
[25] Crowley (1875-1947) was the Master Satanist of the 20th Century.

your soul's intent and transform your soul in the process. The soul is always supposed to be the one in charge, not the personality, which changes with each lifetime.

MIDDLE LETTER IS 'Y'

The middle letter of 'Y' is the same as the first letter 'Y', so read that one. There is a saying that is helpful for you to remember, "Religious people are afraid of going to hell, while spiritual people have lived through hell."

MIDDLE LETTER IS 'Z'

You are one tough character who loves victory. You are prone to prompt decisions, which can cause you to get into trouble, or cause you to not complete your assigned tasks. You are a natural military ruler as you are a warrior who has a talent for controlling other people. However, you would be horrified if someone attempted to control you.

Your soul is a great philosopher, who would learn much from listening to others, yet that is not your way.

Your soul wants you to develop the ability to astral travel and the ability to apologize. A good apology has three parts;

1. Stating what you did wrong, why you understand that your behavior choice was wrong and what you learned from your actions
2. What you'll do differently next time
3. What you are willing to do to make up for the mistake you made.

Your soul is strong and determined. Your challenge is to listen to others and not just do whatever comes into your mind without thought behind it.

CHAPTER 6:
CONSONANT COMBINATIONS

"You are nameless, because those letters grouped together in that familiar form..... carries too much meaning for my capricious heart." Coco J. Ginger

Just as atoms come together to create properties that they didn't have previously, like water made from hydrogen and oxygen, represented as H_2O, letters come together into groups to create characteristics that they didn't have previously. As the letters combine they present greater challenges and more powerful gifts.

We all love to hear about the gifts and may have a natural proclivity to avoid or feel negative about our challenges. However, the more challenges, difficulties, and problems that you encounter in your life indicate the more you will be able to grow, learn and increase your inner power. This is due to being forced to find solutions that work to solve problems. You are being given the opportunity to elaborate on possible solutions by using logical thinking skills. This, in turn, raises your awareness and consciousness. There is a saying, "What doesn't kill you makes you stronger". Thus, your determination can assist you to succeed.

Just as there is polarity in our universe, an up to every down, an inside to every outside, a positive to every negative, there are both challenges and gifts in every name and in the consonant combinations.

The double letters provide double challenges. It means you choose not to waste a moment of this lifetime by idly sitting by. You wished to make this lifetime count. thus you gave yourself an extra challenges.

THE LETTERS 'BR'

You use your charisma, and charm to gain control. You wish to have control even if it means resorting to humiliating others. But you are sly. You don't humiliate publicly, instead you choose to be sly and hide your true goals while you get others to do the humiliation for you.

You can be brutal, or others around you have been brutal to you. Either way, there is bullying in your sphere. You are the bully, or you have been bullied, or both. You have a belief or consciousness of unworthiness, so you may simply choose to suffer silently, but your energy field often attracts those of a "bully" state of consciousness because both victims and perpetrators carry the same energy of unworthiness. Remember, like energy attracts like energy. Bullying cannot be solved by punishment, but by the attainment of a sense of worth within the individual. Your goal, regardless of which side of the fence you reside is to find your own worth, your own value.

The energy that results in being bullied, or

being the bully, is usually carried from past life experiences. It needs to be cleared at it's root, not with medication, but with truth. Your soul wants you to find your own self-worth, and stop the bully energy once and for all.

THE LETTERS 'CH'

Your soul seeks balance and justice. Your need for justice immediately attracts or repels others. Thus, some people will not like you immediately and not know why. You attempt to hide your anger that stems from frustrations, that others are not as attuned as yourself. You crave authority and this causes you to makes things more difficult than they need to be, even though you will succeed.

Your soul wants you to realize that you feel you need to be in charge when you are most afraid because you feel the safest when you are in charge. What would happen if you weren't in charge? Are others just as competent as yourself? What is wrong with not having the most ideal result?

Your soul wants you to realize that just as you are talented, so are others. Just as you can figure out alternative methods to solving problems, so can others. Just because you are fabulous getting things done the right way, so are others. Your goal is to allow others to take the lead once in a while and not be afraid of the outcomes. Your goal is to learn to trust others as your trust yourself.

THE LETTERS 'CHR'

Your personality demands attention because you have excellent energy, and want to do what is right, per your own definition of what is right. Your soul wants you to enjoy being a strong leader without resorting to egoic activities to get attention, or falling into your ego's trap and ending up with a deity complex.

You are here to become gracious. This means no whining when things don't go your way. This means no complaining, without doing something to change what you are complaining about. Your soul wishes for you to become compassionate, starting with yourself. Your goal is to do well so that you and others benefit.

THE LETTERS 'CL'

You feel things intensely, yet you frequently hide your emotions such that you appear calm on the outside although you are anything but calm on the inside. Your emotions can run rampant, especially when you decide you must prove their worth to others, or when you temporarily do not approve of yourself.

Your soul realizes that you find it difficult to follow rules that make no sense to you. That is why you prefer to make up your own rules and to follow only those rules you consider legitimate and your own rules. You are quite innovative in your approach to life.

Your soul wants you to live by your own standard and not anyone else's standards. That is once you have followed normal rules and laws and have lived enough of your life to be in a position to know right from wrong. Your soul wants you to be ethical in your choices and succumb to following both man's laws and universal laws. Your goal is to help change the laws that don't make sense to you, and get them off of the books for everyone, so that we don't become a lawless society with everyone making up their own rules.

THE LETTERS 'CR'

You have internal conflict as you want to be in charge of others, and simultaneously, to be rebellious when others try to be in charge of you. You are different than most of the people that you meet as you are a non-conformist. Actually, you could organize and lead a successful rebellion.

Your soul is adventurous and wants to explore alternative ways of accomplishing familiar tasks. Your soul wants to experience enough differences in methodologies that you can know what is real, and what isn't, so that your internal conflict diminishes. Your goal is to find inner peace some time during your life.

THE LETTERS 'DD'

You do a great job living up to other's expectations of you. Your soul feels this is doubly boring and that you can easily fall into a regiment. Your soul wants you to experiment with life so that you are comfortable when in new situations. Your soul is highly appreciative of religion and what it has to offer.

Explore what works for you. Your goal is to make the religious understandings that you have come alive for you in your life. How do you incorporate your religious and moral understandings into your life?

THE LETTERS 'DR'

You have worked hard, been goal oriented, and earned respect from others for the knowledge that you carry. Your soul is blessed and wants you to share your knowledge to help others. The knowledge you have worked so hard to obtain is not just for you. Your goal is not to become ungrateful or entitled because of your success.

THE LETTERS 'FF'

You tend to be a collector of things and hopefully your collecting does not cause you to become a hoarder, keeping things well beyond their usefulness. Your soul recognizes your style of being tenacious and methodical so that you are steadily achieving. You are resourceful and frugal and loyal to loved ones. When planning your future you need to see the whole picture or plan prior to starting on the parts.

Your soul wants you to learn important lessons. They are not to hoard as that speaks to not trusting the universe to provide. Your soul wants you to learn how to not take advantage of friendships where you become entitled to what they have, possibly borrowing items frequently enough that after a while you consider the item yours. Your soul wants to learn to be the leader in your home without becoming a bureaucrat and ordering your family members on what to do.

Your goal is to remain honest; to remain humble; to remain loyal to your friends without taking advantage of your friendship. Lastly, your goal is to learn to trust that you will be alright so that no aspect of greed tempts you.

THE LETTERS 'FR'

You have learned how to hide your true self under a veil of charm. Your award winning smile, your persuasive speech, and your spontaneity disarms others.

Your soul knows you could help many find their way. Your goal is not to become cheap or stingy, or scam others as they find your charm irresistible. Your goal is to use your charm for the good of all and not for personal, temporary, illusionary benefits.

THE LETTERS 'GG'

You have a larger than life personality. People remember you. You can be intense, irritating, and innovative. You've been dealt a double edged sword, since you have been given intelligence and the power of influence.

You can be a force for change and contribute to others being willing to look at things from a different perspective. Your goal is to use your creativity to encourages change in others, while remaining flexible yourself. Your soul gets bored when things are on the even keel for too long. So, your goal is not to use alcohol or some other drug to numb yourself to how the world currently is, or to escape from the world. Your goal is to shine and become a beacon of light.

THE LETTERS 'GH'

In order to grow people have to be willing to change. As people get older, they become more set in their ways. Hence, one more reason for reincarnation. However, these are the very reasons you are so needed as you are an instigators, and assist others to grow and change.

Your soul wishes for you to be aware of the consequences of your actions on others though, because, at times, you can be quite oblivious, not noticing what you've caused. Your soul is wanting to change the world to something more agreeable to your understanding of utopia.

Your goal is to be aware of all of your actions and their ensuing consequences. This way you can take responsibility for your choices and not blame something or someone else for your predicaments.

THE LETTERS 'GL'

You are overly concerned with rules and prone to depression when you get discouraged that others are not following the rules. Your soul wishes you to use your comedic humor to assist you when you become overly vigilant, as that is how you retreat and protect yourself.

Your goal is to enjoy the finer things in life without becoming overly cautious when going forward. Be watchful that you don't choose to bury your disappointments about life in the wine bottle or an equivalent bottle.

THE LETTERS 'GR'

You have combined your gifts of innovation and spiritual knowledge and coupled these with rebelliousness. This translates into the willingness to fight for what one believes. You are a warrior, and willing to die for what you believe in.

Your soul wants you to realize that life is precious and unless it is a sacred duty, not to throw your life away for some trivial reason. Your goal is to use your innovative self to solve problems in such a way that war is not necessary.

THE LETTERS 'HL'

You can be at the mercy of others or others can be at your mercy. Your soul is here to learn what real mercy is. Mercy includes being able to forgive, having compassion and leniency towards others. Your goal is to have forbearance and grow in your magnanimity.

THE LETTERS 'HLS'

You need to be careful not to misuse your freedoms, as it can appear that you lack strength of will or you lack common sense. Your soul wants you to be aware of when you misuse your energy to self-sabotage what you know to be the right action to take.

Your soul wants you to strengthen your moral convictions so that when challenged you will not find it difficult to avoid succumbing to inappropriate sexual advances from others. Your soul wants you to learn how to use your energy wisely so your energy isn't wasted on negative thoughts. Your goal is to learn to stay focused and positive with a high level of integrity.

THE LETTERS 'HM'

You are religiously minded to the point where you can be a religious fanatic. Your soul knows how important it is to have a relationship with God and encourages that. Your goal is to embody your religious beliefs without dismissing anyone else's beliefs or thinking that their beliefs, when different from your own, don't have any merit.

Your soul wishes for you to learn that there are many pathways to God as God is multifaceted. Your goal is to learn how to accept other people's beliefs are just as important to them and just as valuable as your beliefs are to you.

THE LETTERS 'HN'

You are loyal, easy to love, beloved and can be divinely chosen. With so many gifts, it would be easy to become egotistical. Be careful not to use your talents in such a way that you become devious to get what you want. This would cause you to become unfaithful and taint your beliefs about God.

Instead, your soul wants you to be dependable, so that others can rely on you and your word becomes the gold bond of trustworthiness. Your goal is to stay beloved and through actions, not just words, let others know why you are so beloved.

THE LETTERS 'KR'

Your personality can be confused, pushy, with aggressive energy that often displays itself as hard on the outside and soft on the inside. You feel most important when you are subjugated to an authority figure as you excel at following orders and doing things the way you are asked to get them done.

Your soul desires for you to not only be good at your job, but to separate yourself from your boss and the directions enough to think for yourself. Just because you are grateful to be hired, does not mean that everything being done in the job is kosher. Your goal is to develop and keep a sense of self that is not defined by others.

THE LETTERS 'LB'

You are naturally delightful, simply charming, due to the pleasant way you have about you. You can become famous in this lifetime if so desired. Your soul wants you to enjoy your hard earned dharma that you have. Your goal is to use your dharma wisely in a service capacity, and not for silliness or guilty pleasures for yourself.

THE LETTERS 'LD'

You frequently felt misunderstood or unappreciated in your youth, as things didn't go as you would have wished. This feeling of lack causes you to have a temper that appears sporadically and can catch loved ones off guard. Your personality has learned how to bury grief, yet your soul wants you to be able to process your grief. You are good with mechanical things, are street smart, and have a tendency to be a martyr.

Your soul wants you to uncomplicate your life, to learn to use your conservative views to simplify your positions that you hold so dear to your heart. Your goal is to let go, and see what happens, knowing you can handle whatever that is.

THE LETTERS 'LK'

You are mechanically inclined, yet routine in your thinking. You tend to think what could be, versus what currently is. This is a great skill as it assists you in seeing beyond what others see. You are able to see how to improve the world versus letting the world be how it currently is. You have this incredible passionate about life, yet amazingly, lack emotional involvement in being attached to life.

Your soul wants you to keep your self-confidence and use it, alone with your natural leadership abilities, and logical step-by-step methodology to progress through life. It does not want you to become mechanical in nature, but to explore alternatives. Your goal is to make a leap of faith and trust that you will land on your feet. Lead your unconventional life in the true spirit of freedom.

THE LETTERS 'LL'

Your personality is a mixed bag. On the one hand, your proclivity is to be a superb writer given some basic training in grammar and how to write. On the other hand you have a short fuse attached to your temper, you are domineering, prone to learning the hard way; and a person who doesn't feel loved enough.

Your soul loves children and animals. Your soul also loves stability and to to be right the first time. However, you can be manipulative when feeling out of control in order to get the stability you so crave. Your goal is to trust, versus to doubt, when making decisions, and to use unconventional thinking patterns to get things done. You are talented, and can use your writings to persuade others in their thinking. Decide what goal you wish to aim towards so that you can truly be successful.

THE LETTERS 'LM'

You come across as initially shy, but that is only until your confidence kicks in. You have gotten used to being passive aggressive to get your needs met. Your ability to plot and plan well exceeds most. You can scheme and hold your own.

Your soul wants you to use your skills to build up a society and not to tear any part of it down. Your soul wants you to stand for high morals and ethics in all of your endeavors.

Your goal is to accomplish much, so that you can be promoted to high places and use your influence to remind others to do well creating win-win situations.

THE LETTERS 'LS'

You can earn a good living on your own. Your life is uncomplicated and you like to keep it that way. Your athletic ability, productivity, and intuitive sense of people causes you to be a favorite among your peers.

Your life would be perfect if it wasn't for the problems that you do have of getting and maintaining loyalty from your significant other. Your significant other can be overly willful.

Your soul wants you to learn how to negotiate the rough spots and support others as you wish they would support you. Your soul wants you to rise to the occasion and do what is necessary for your family. In doing so, you'll rise the understanding of the people around you.

Your goal is to smile and put yourself second. Swallow pride and support your family. Find the gift in the deceit; what did you learn? Can you work your way through it? Your soul goal for you this lifetime is to learn how to truly forgive. Forgive the offender and yourself and those who were honest enough to tell you the truth, even when you did not want to hear it.

THE LETTERS 'LT'

You take everything to the extreme, you do

what you like and don't do what you don't like doing. You have an active imagination or fantasy life; are extremely competent or you are incompetent to the extreme, as it is either excess or total abstinence.

Your soul realizes that you will blossom later in life, while being awkward or socially inept during their school years. Your soul wants you to use this to develop your interests and to attempt different things versus deciding with your mind what you'll do well and what you won't do well.

Your goal is to try a variety of things and then decide what you like and what, with practice, you'll do well. Your goal is to learn moderation.

THE LETTERS 'LV'

You have a tendency, or disposition, to become a martyr, as your self-confidence is tied to your belief of your sex appeal. You martyr yourself to boast your confidence hoping others will like you more because of your ability to self-sacrifice. That is the same reason that you have moments where you show off your flamboyant self, all in the name of getting attention.

Your soul wants you to gain self-confidence without becoming a martyr. Your soul wishes you to know that you have value; that you are good enough without resorting to antics.

Your goal is to do activities that build your confidence so that you don't have to do anything that ostentatious to gain acceptance from your peers. Your goal is to see the intrinsic value that you have and that you are.

THE LETTERS LL

You find it hard to make decisions even though you have confidence and realize your self-worth. This is an exploratory life, exploring what different situations feel like, exploring options on how to handle various situations so that everyone wins.

Your soul wants you to experiment, and

experience the different things that life has to offer, and then write about those experiences. You have the talent to not only be a good writer, but a great writer.

Your goal is to write, and express yourself, after having a myriad of experiences, so that you develop your writing skills and simultaneously learn to enjoy new adventures.

THE LETTERS 'LW'

You have confidence, which has come from developing your knowledge and turning it into wisdom. Your soul wants you to be pleased with your progress without becoming arrogant. Your goal is to use your confidence to assist others and not to lord it over others.

THE LETTERS 'MM'

You naturally whine in such a way that others

immediately respond. You can be sly, and use your looks to your advantage. You can be by bossy in order to gain an outcome that you preplanned.

Your soul wants you to not whine, and to realize that using your God given assets to get what is not rightfully yours is not appropriate and has consequences for which your soul is held accountable. Your goal is to use your mind, not your physical assets to get ahead. Your goal is also to be grateful for what you have instead of not being satisfied and always wanting more. Also, be careful of wanting what rightfully isn't yours, like another person's spouse.

THE LETTERS 'NN'

You are incredibly organized in one's area of interest. You share your knowledge and are a competitive workaholic, even as you do not take direction from others well. You are well grounded and creating money is important

THE LETTERS 'NC'

You are capable of holding grudges, which you use as a motivating factor to help you overcome tremendous odds. Your soul wants you to realize that you are capable of so much more than what you perceive that you can. Your goal is not to hold a grudge; instead to be able to see situations from someone else's point of view.

THE LETTERS 'NCH'

Thoughts can be bad enough, but not nearly as bad as when actions are taken based on those thoughts. You have a tough challenge as you wish to make things right, or get even, and make the other person pay for what you perceived they did wrong. As such, you are capable of committing heinous, despicable acts.

Your soul urges you to ask where your anger originated. Seek to find the cause so that your actions are not misplaced. Your goal is to conquer your emotions and do your reflection so that you stop yourself prior to committing horrible acts. Remember that your choices create karma and dharma.

THE LETTERS 'ND'

You are quite observant of human behavior, balanced in your masculinity and femininity, and spiritually oriented. You have so much going for you. You are most comfortable when in control of self, and responsible to others, but not for others. Somehow, you feel like you don't always fit in with the crowd, that somehow you are different.

Your soul wants you to take that feeling and make it work for you. Be you, remembering that you don't need to fit in with the crowd. Being authentic is so much better. Your goal is to be an excellent networker, a talented leader in diverse fields and to be yourself at all times.

THE LETTERS 'NR'

You are both altruistic and artistic in your endeavors because you have a high sense of community duty. This also causes you to be philanthropic when you are older. You are far sighted in your decisions about today's problems.

Your soul knows you are gifted in many areas and wishes you to use your gifts for the good of the entire community. In order to do so, your soul is asking that you put others first, while still including yourself in the group.

You have so much going for you that you will be tempted to allow the ego to reign. Your goal is to stay community minded, and not to become egotistical.

THE LETTERS 'PH'

You are either a staunch, fanatically honest person, or a person who lies to self, one extreme or the other. You do not feel that you fit into society. Either way, you find it hard to connect to others personally, on an intimate level.

Your soul would like you to find where you are special and what is your area where people will appreciate your differences. You don't feel like you fit in for a reason. Explore those feelings so that you can discover why you are different, and how you can use that area can be of service to others.

Your goal is to create win-win situations, and to use your will to stand out from the crowd. You have a gift. Your goal is to find it and use it.

THE LETTERS 'PR'

You have an inner toughness that is hidden by your outer composure. You are able to hide your feelings in the line of duty while staying level headed. This lessens potential dramas which could occur if you failed to stay collected and in control of your emotions.

Your soul wishes you to test yourself so that you master your emotions. Your goal is to stay level headed regardless of the situations that you find yourself experiencing.

THE LETTERS 'RB'

You are a typical spirit experiencing being human and as such you will spend this lifetime learning about the importance of being truthful, learning how being rebellious can have its advantages and disadvantages.

Your soul understands the world due to your native intelligence. Your soul wishes you to be appreciative of the great range of personalities instead of being critical of others.

Your goal is to not become conceited, or insecurities, so that you feel fragile instead of being domineering and enjoying being in a human body.

THE LETTERS 'RC'

You can be considered a slow starter in some areas. It is not that you are slow, but that you wish only to make commitments that are viable and that you can keep.

Your soul has lacked insight or vision,

preferring to maintain the status quo. Your soul is more comfortable when in control of the surrounding issues, as it fears unpredictable, erratic behavior.

Your goal is to monitor your own behavior so you don't become that which your soul fears.

THE LETTERS 'RD'

You are drawn to imitation, as you are not yet awake to your own Divine Nature, and so have no real sense of self worth. This state of consciousness frequently lashes out though violence because you fee like you are missing something that others have within themselves. You feel left out, unworthy, and rejected. This creates an emotional temper within you that can suddenly explode for apparently no reason. The real reason is that you sit on your emotions until you can no longer contain them. You are frequently drawn to positions of authority where you are able to act out your frustrations and need for power legally.

Your soul is wonderful. You have a good heart, can be exceptionally kind, and seek maturity.

Your goal is to make large amounts of people consider you their hero without losing them due to having critical disregard for others that don't perform up to your standards. You are subtle sometimes when being direct is better and bold and full of vigor and vim when sometimes being subtle is more appropriate. Your goal is to know which is better and when to use each approach for the maximum benefit to your goals.

THE LETTERS 'RH'

You're curiosity about life leads you to explore unknown areas. You so appreciate life that you end up having a magnetic pull that captivates other people and pulls them to you like a magnet.

Your soul wishes you to use this energy to attract people to you for positive reinforcement. It is so easy for people to get negative and to let their fears dominate. Your challenge is to stay positive.

Your goal is to keep looking for, and taking advantage of opportunities, without falling into having sexual delusions or acting out your fears.

THE LETTERS 'RG'

This letter combination represents a great gift of being interested in things that others are not. You can discover things within yourself that causes you to question what you have been taught and this leads you forward to explore and look with fresh eyes.

The challenge with this combination is not to consider others stupid, or incompetent, or to get frustrated, or mad because others do not see what you see. Another trigger can be when others do not share the knowledge that you seek, or teach you what you wish to learn.

Instead of blaming others along your quest for knowledge, your goal is to go within, and learn to live in conjunction with the Universe. That is how your soul finds the peace it seeks.

THE LETTERS 'RK'

You have traditional thinking which is quite powerful. You enjoy an exchange of ideas as long as they are conventional. Your soul wishes to challenge you to increase how often you use your imagination and your creativity.

Your goals are to return every item you borrow, exchange ideas without claiming someone else's idea as your own, and to continue to grow stronger over time.

THE LETTERS 'RL'

Your greatest attribute is your ability to be self depreciating. Your soul wants to challenge you in the area of finances and thoughts. Your goal is to take care of yourself financially and to control your mind as it can rationalize or justify anything.

THE LETTERS 'RM'

You tend to be extremely talkative, and prefer to be in charge, even as you have a hard time keeping that position as don't want your authority to be questioned or tested.

Your soul wants you to talk a bit less and listen a bit more. Others have good suggestions that you may be missing. When one questions your authority, please realize that they are wanting to understand more and it is not a personal attack on you.

Your goal is to learn how to remain calm under fire so that you can think quickly and accurately. Remember, what you believe to be true is not necessarily how everyone else sees the same situation.

THE LETTERS 'RR'

You need reflection time to make sure that you stay balanced, hence you often find yourself alone. Perhaps you prefer to work alone in order to get your alone time as this time is so crucial to you.

Your soul wishes for you to stay in balance, to stay focused and not to become a victim of self imposed limitations.

Your goal is to stay affable, and not become obnoxious due to lack of time alone, to use your ability to be charming in a positive manner and to develop accurate discernment.

THE LETTERS 'RT'

You are challenged by the need for perfection, and are invited to realize that you already are perfect in this moment, just as all others have the potential to recognize their own perfection. Acknowledge the divine spark within you is already perfect. Remember perfect is not a stagnate state but one that is ever changing and ever growing.

You are becoming that which you are becoming, and allow yourself to grow and be. The search for perfectionism starts by going inside, and is not outside of you. You are this loving divine essence that is an all-encompassing feeling of knowing that it is all right to be you. You are perfect the way you are just as others are perfect just the way they are. By accepting this understanding and the love that comes with it, you may assist in transferring this acceptance of self to others.

Your biggest challenge is not to superimpose your definition of perfection onto others. Instead, allow your acceptance of self to permeate and create an acceptance of others for exactly how they are.

THE LETTERS 'RTM'

You are amicable, and mature beyond your years. You take what you like to do and do it well and to the extreme. Conversely, what you don't like to do, you procrastinate and wish you could avoid the task altogether.

Your soul loves the fact that you can have mindless abandonment; that you don't have to be focused on work all of the time, even as you excel at what you do.

Your goal is to balance your work time with your play time. You may even consider redefining what you consider fun as often work and play are considered the same thing.

THE LETTERS 'SC'

You are a friendly loner, bright yet humble, and calm in tough situations. You are also well mannered, and pleasant.

Your soul wishes you to remember not to become disrespectful, or to take advantage of others and then stab them in the back.

Your goal is to be loyal to your own goals without hurting others in the process. Please listen well and stay compassionate while pursuing your goals.

THE LETTERS 'SCH'

There are times when you can be stubborn, and other times when you flip that stubbornness into persistence. You are able to figure out ways around rules, usually outsmarting people in authority.

Your soul wants you to take advantage of other people's knowledge so that you begin to get comfortable getting out of your own way. Your goal is to trust others enough that you are willing to learn from them.

THE LETTERS 'SH'

Your soul desires freedom from rules and tyranny more than anything else. Give yourself permission to live without the superficial barriers imposed by governments, religions and institutions. You are a free thinker and are only happy when following the Universal Laws. You are not a fan of being limited by mankind's insidious rules. Your challenge is to find a way to live within mankind's rules while simultaneously dedicating yourself to following all of the Universal Laws of which you are aware.

How do you merge the two without falling into the trap that rules are made for others and not for you? Remember, the choice is yours when you can break rules. However, there are consequences for breaking both mankind's rules and Universal Laws. Thus, it is important to choose wisely, accepting the possible consequences, if you are choosing to break any rules.

Remember, mankind's rules are there as guideposts until you can discern for yourself the necessity of any such rule. You will have the discernment to know when it is safe to break mankind's rules. Your challenge is to create your life of freedom, while always adhering to both the cultural and universal laws.

THE LETTERS 'SR'

Your are unstoppable as long as you stay focused and don't procrastinate. Your soul wants you to take advantage of the gifts you have been given and accomplish as much as you can. Your soul wants you to focus on all of the goals you have in your name and accomplish all of them. Don't get sidetracked by your need to rescue others. You'll do best when you follow your own truth and not someone else's.

THE LETTERS 'SS'

People might consider you noisy, wanting to know all about someone else's business, but you only want information about other people so that you can be there if they require assistance. Thus, you feel better when you are well informed.

Your soul wants you to know the difference between being there for someone and rescuing. Rescuing gains you karma, while being there earns you dharma. Rescuing means you are assisting by doing something for the other person that he can do for himself. So, unintentionally you are saying that the other person is not good enough. You have established him as weaker than you. That is why you get karma for that action.

However, when you can listen well, really hearing what is being said, and then ask question to cause additional thinking or make suggestions based on what you heard, without attempting to direct which suggestion is accepted, if any, that is helpful and creates dharma.

Your goal is to listen, and respond appropriately, without rescuing anyone. As tough as that is for you, know it is possible.

THE LETTERS 'ST'

You can be incredibly stubborn, which is you getting in your own way. You also can be incredibly persistent which means you can finish long, arduous tasks, like getting through medical school, and not dropping out. Your soul wishes you to use your energy on the persistent side and not waste this valuable energy by being stubborn. Your goal is to master all aspects of this stubborn/persistent energy.

THE LETTERS 'STR'

You are lighthearted and so pleasant to be around. Your soul wants you to uplift the spirits of the people around you. Your goal is to also uplift yourself in the process.

THE LETTERS 'TH'

You have a tendency to agitate others, picking on them to get their reaction as you feel insignificant in some way and have learned to increase your power by confronting others and making arguments out of little things so that you can regain your power. You are afraid that someone might see how insignificant you feel, and so you hide behind a mask of your own creation extolling your power, your creativeness, your need to have more power than others. That is what keeps you safe.

Therefore you want to be on top of everything, the one in charge, or on your way to the top. Fearing you won't be the best; you can refuse to even start something, as failure would devastate you by reconfirming your fears of being nothing, and of not having value. So, it is all or nothing in your world.

Your soul wants you to realize how important you are, even when you do nothing, and how much you have to contribute when you are doing something. Your soul wants you to know that you have value just by being you. The Creator did not make a mistake when you were made.

Your goal is to learn how to appreciate your existence. That having a human body is marvelous and to appreciate how your body extends and compliments you. Exercise is the remedy for you when feeling deprived, or any kind of angst. Your mission is to come into appreciation of your very existence.

THE LETTERS 'NTH'

These letters represent the fear of commitment, being self absorbed, and taking things to the extreme in one area of life. Your soul wants you to find balance in your life and learn how to be concerned with the whole, versus just the part that is you. Your goal is to trust the universe enough so there is no cause to be afraid, and so you don't feel you need to use extreme measures to keep yourself save.

THE LETTERS 'TR'

You are a dichotomy as you want to get things done and yet can lack awareness in how to get things done either efficiently, correctly or how it'll affect others. Your soul wants you to navigate your way through obstacles well enough so that you become highly successful. Your goal is to find a way to be safe with your feelings whereby you can then focus on your work. This is the way for you to be incredibly successful.

THE LETTERS 'TT'

You can be materialistic; a workaholic or

lazy to boot; a non-conformist; individualistic; spiritual; highly successful or in jail. You do what you want to do and definitely don't want to do what you don't like to do.

Your soul wishes for you to find a way to experience more things, especially those you initially would prefer to avoid. Your goal is to have as many varied experiences as possible and to become okay with doing your best in fields you would initially choose to not try.

THE LETTERS 'TTH'

You can definitely be hard headed, absolutely intense, resilient and being able to land on one's feet regardless of hard situations, besides having athletic ability that is the envy of others.

Your soul wants you to lighten up and not be quite so hard headed, yet to stay focused and intense. It is your intensity that causes you to succeed. Your goal is not to do anything in its extreme without due safety precautions first. In your private life, do your best to find balance.

THE LETTERS 'TN'

You can be obsessive-compulsive in your behavior. This can be used positively or negatively. Either way, you will gain the public's attention. Your soul wants you to contain and cure your obsessive-compulsive impulses and to use your gifts in a positive manner. Your goal is not to let the public's attention cause you to become egotistical.

THE LETTERS 'TX' AND 'TZ'

You are highly sensitive in your physical body as well as being highly intuitive to the point where occasionally you feel as if spirits are around you. You seek to discover for yourself how things truly are by living life to the fullest possible and seeing what transpires.

Freedom, in every manner of the word, is what your soul seeks as it does not wish to be limited by anyone or anything. Your soul seeks universal wisdom, not the everyday variety. In doing so, it does not appreciate anyone telling you what you need to do, or how things are in a definitive way.

Your soul craves adventure and entering into new territory so that it may collect as many experiences as possible. Yes, you can learn from others, yet your pull is to take the information that has been shared with you and test it to see if it also works for you.

Your goal, or challenge, is to be able to create for yourself an adventurous life, one well explored, without lowering yourself to another's standards in order to fit into to their perception of what life should be. Real stability comes from understanding yourself. True freedom comes from being you. Remember, life is an experience. Constrain the ego so that you do not become deceived or attract false friends to yourself.

THE LETTERS 'WH'

The Tree of Life explains why things are the way they are and is the mystical missing piece that was so well guarded in ancient times. The Kabbala does its best to explain the mysteries behind The Tree of Life. In ancient times, mystical schools were set up to share the knowledge represented by this Tree.

The greatest challenge though is not to academically understand the Tree, but to assimilate this knowledge into daily life. Today is no different. How do you assimilate and become the knowledge that you hold so that it expresses itself through your every action? The good news is that when you do your best, the laws of the Universe take care of the rest.

You judge yourself harshly when you make the same mistake twice. You would rather make brand new delicious errors than repeat one as it indicates you failed to learn your lesson from the first mistake as you want to advance mankind. Repeating previous errors is considered an obstacle that slows you down.

Most often, you use your wisdom in pursuit of things good, light and spiritual. Your soul wants you to use caution in your pursuit of knowledge, to be able to change discord into harmony, and to grow in your humanitarianism.

Your goal is not to fall into the trap of having impatience with other's stupidity or impatience when they do not catch on fast enough as this causes you to become quarrelsome and stubborn. When you buy into the belief that others are stupid and whoa is the world is when you become susceptible to depression.

SUMMARY

We are not limited to our destiny; rather our own actions determine our fate. Remember our contract for this lifetime is directing, but not confirming, the destiny of individuals and nations. We are directed to create from passion and joy, as our intent creates the building blocks within the matrix. Remember, it takes courage to seek the spiritual path and to stay on it, especially since the spiritual path demands a high level of integrity.

CHAPTER 7: VOWEL DIPHTHONGS

"Human beings not even worthy of their own names attack the character of others." Michael Horn

Vowels represent emotions that are felt, but not necessarily said. We connect to one another on the emotional level, so vowels let us know how well we will interact. Each vowel has its own attributes. When we combine the vowels, as in diphthongs, we get more expansive connections. Said another way, we connect in a deeper, more pure way than we were able to connect previously. Our emotions intensify with diphthongs and, occasionally, so do our inner conflicts. Remember to check each vowel individually first in the other chapter prior to reading these, as these diphthongs are in addition to the vowel's singular meaning.

THE 'A' DIPHTHONGS

THE LETTERS 'AA'

You are an overachievers who continually attempts to prove to yourself your own worth and value. This is because you don't know your own value. Your soul wants you to realize that you have value simply because you exist and that God does not make mistakes. Your goal is to value yourself, be able to accept a complement and see your own value.

THE LETTERS 'AE'

You strive for balance between your mental and emotional feelings, often not knowing which one to trust or act upon, as you are in conflict within yourself not knowing which one to trust more, your heart or your head. Your soul wants you to distinguish between your mental reasoning skills and where your heart takes you. Your goal is to trust your mental skills and allow your mind to dominate.

THE LETTERS 'AI'

You can be overly sensitive, a bit lovelorn, and are highly protective of loved ones. You can also be thin skinned due to being overly sensitive, somewhat needy, as well as a bit pushy. All of this is the result of your attempt to get your needs met. Bottom line: it is easy for you to feel hurt emotionally and/or physically.

Your soul wants you to toughen up, to realize you are not alone and to know that you can get your needs met without being aggressive. Your goal is to not take everything personally, instead to realize that everyone is simply trying to survive to the best of their own knowledge. Use your knowledge to guide you to your solutions.

THE LETTERS 'AO'

You are unstoppable, determined, and goal oriented. Your soul is dynamic and strong and wishes you to use these skills in your own growth and to build upon them. Your goal is not to become conceited along the way.

THE LETTERS 'AU'

You have a magnetic personality, and you are dependable during a crisis. However, you evade change as much as possible as you get comfortable with the way things are and don't wish for them to change. Thus you procrastinate hoping that helps things stay the way they are.

Your soul wants you to trust that change is inevitable and to become comfortable with both the idea of change and its actuality. Your goal is to remain flexible and adaptable to the extent that changes are no longer uncomfortable.

THE LETTERS 'AY'

You can do anything you put your mind to do. The trick is to stay focused. Nothing can stop you when you stay focused. Your soul is a very old soul and as such, doesn't want to waste time getting off track. Your goal is to figure out the reason you are here, and then finish what the reasons showed you, so that you can be done.

THE 'E' DIPHTHONGS

THE LETTERS 'EA'

You are an emotional being and you strive for balance between your mental and emotional feelings; often not knowing which one to trust or act upon, as you are in conflict within yourself not knowing which one to trust more, your heart or your head. Your soul wants you to distinguish between your mental reasoning skills and where your heart takes you. Your goal is to trust your heart and allow your emotions to dominate. This way you can become aware of how others see you and make it easier to separate your private life from your public life.

THE LETTERS 'EAU'

You wear rose colored glasses, and as such have a tendency to believe your own propaganda. Your soul wants you to realize what is real, versus what is illusion. Your goal is to see reality for what it is and not what you'd prefer it to be.

THE LETTERS 'EE'

You are so empathetic that it is easy for you

to confuse other people's emotions with your own. Your soul is open to loving and expresses that with every fiber of your being. Your goal is to stay loving, separating what you sense others are feeling from that which you are feeling. This way you can experience your emotions without having other emotions intrude upon you. You want to feel the extremes of emotions and learn how to be comfortable with all emotions, not just the pleasant ones.

THE LETTERS 'EI'

You have always had to depend on yourself for emotional support as you have so often felt as if family was not there for you. To support yourself you have learned to take risks and you also have experienced extreme loneliness. Your soul is asking you to become a generator for your own energy. Your goal is to become so solid in your ability to understand the world and support yourself emotionally, that you are able to do this for others also.

THE LETTERS 'EO'

You have been blessed with self-confidence, determination, assertiveness and are a good problem solver. Your soul wants you to use your skills to dispel disharmony in yourself and others. Your goal is be a mediator in all that you do.

THE LETTERS 'EU'

You are drawn to imitation, as you are not yet awake to your own Divine Nature, and so you have no real sense of self worth. Your state of consciousness frequently causes you to lash out through violence because you feel like you are missing something that others have within themselves. You feel left out, unworthy, and rejected. You are playful, flirtatious, possessive, and have an insatiable need for love. You have temper challenges as you are easily frustrated when you are not able to control your emotions.

This creates an emotional temper within you that can suddenly explode for apparently no reason. The real reason is that you sit on your emotions until you can no longer contain them. You are frequently drawn to positions of authority where you are able to act out your frustrations and need for power legally.

Your soul wants you to realize that God doesn't make mistakes and that you have value, if for no other reason than you exist. Your soul wants you to learn how to forgive yourself for participation in painful events.

Your goal is to master your emotions to the extent that your temper doesn't flare up or you become out of control. Your goal is to satisfy your need for love in positive ways versus self righteous ways.

THE LETTERS 'EY'

You have a tendency to rescue others as you love to fight for the underdog. This can cause you to feel ecstasy when you succeed and depressed when you don't. Your soul loves everyone and feels badly when it perceives others hurting. Your goal is not to be gullible when dealing with what you perceive to be an underdog. Your goal is also to look at why you have the need to rescue others. What is lacking in you that you need to be considered a hero?

THE 'I' DIPHTHONGS

THE LETTERS 'IA'

You have a tendency to be altruistic, and are definitely humanity oriented. Your soul works hard to support and be of service to the family of man. Your goal is not to sacrifice yourself in order to help others.

THE LETTERS 'IE'

You are emotionally healthy, which allows you to feel secure and take risks. You feel safe and protected, and thus reach out to other people and allowing them space to feel as if nothing can harm them.

Your soul is tenacious and simply doesn't give up, regardless of the circumstances. Your goal is to trust the universe so that you can assist others to trust the universe and know, without any doubt, that things will work out in the long run. Keep believing in people.

THE LETTERS 'II'

You are an example of sheer perfection, at least in your own view of how life works. Your soul wants you to realize that others are just as wonderful as you. Your goal is not to become enamored with yourself.

THE LETTERS 'IO'

You are a natural leader as people feel comfortable coming to you for answers. However, you have conflict within yourself on how to lead. Should you lead by example, by being a friend, by being authoritarian, or by copying what your predecessors did? Your soul wants you to figure out your own way of leading. Your goal is to lead without seeking to draw attention to yourself.

THE LETTERS 'IU'

You fight for your own beliefs, as you have developed your own perspective. You can be a powerful persuader. Your soul wants you to keep learning, so that your beliefs can grow and change as your understandings develop. Your goal is to stay flexible so that you can adapt, and incorporate new information into your belief structure.

THE 'O' DIPHTHONGS

THE LETTERS 'OU'

You are worldly, and enjoy being politically correct. You also have an offbeat sense of humor which is delightful. Your soul wants you to keep your splendid humor and use it to lighten up situations when others are feeling down. Your goal is to stay positive and to keep seeing the silver lining in all situations.

THE LETTERS 'OUI'

You have a well rounded perspective, plus a directed purpose, as you feel as if you are on a mission. You like routine, so others may consider you boring. Your soul wants you to stay well rounded and on task to what you feel your purpose is. Your goal is not to let others take you off task.

THE LETTERS 'OUIE'

You have added time issues to the challenges described above in 'OUI'. Your soul wants you to manage your time better so that you can realize the gift that time truly is. Your goal is to plan your work and work your plan while not allowing others to take you off task.

THE LETTERS 'OY'

You are a late bloomer who can become an amazing leader who is both powerful and talented. Your soul wants you to use your abilities for the good of the whole focusing on others and not on yourself. Your goal is to gain pleasure from the good that you do and not crave the limelight in the process.

THE 'U' DIPHTHONGS

THE LETTERS 'UA'

You are mature beyond your chronological years so much so that others consider you a master teacher. Your soul wants you to keep growing and not to rest on your laurels. Your goal is to share your knowledge with others without considering yourself somehow better than others or as a savior.

THE LETTERS 'UE'

You have the fabulous ability to laugh at yourself, and as such are rarely solemn. Your soul wants you to stay cheerful. Your goal is to stay humble so that you may keep laughing.

THE LETTERS 'UI'

You are social, but underneath can be shy. You will do what is necessary to preserve your status. Your soul wants you to stay honest and to think of others while preserving self, and how your actions may affect them. Your goal is to let go of your self-doubt so that there is no need to worry about your status.

THE 'Y' DIPHTHONGS

THE LETTERS 'YA'

You can be a bit cocky, somewhat abrasive, and you expect high payoffs for small endeavors. Your soul wants you to tame yourself so that you are both more pleasant and reasonable. Your goal is to become more compassionate and understanding of others' needs, balancing your desire to be overpaid for work instead of requesting a reasonable amount commensurate with the work you have performed.

THE LETTERS 'YO'

You have a strong ego, you follow the rules,

are exacting, and power hungry. Your soul wants you to keep your ego in check, as well as your need for power. Your goal is to keep following mankind's rules as well as universal laws.

THE LETTERS 'YU'

You are like royalty, charming and lovable. Your soul asks that you use your charming ways to benefit others and not take advantage of them. Your goal is to stay benevolent in your thoughts.

CHAPTER 8:
MIXED SYNTACTIC SOUNDS

"Every name is real. That's the nature of names." Jerry Spinelli in <u>Stargirl</u>

Mixed syntactic sounds represent our religious and spiritual understandings as well as what is most important to us in this lifetime. Let us read a quote from the website Quora to better understand the difference between religion and spirituality.

"A religious person predominantly focuses attention from the framework of the small self. Rituals and prayers orient the mind towards conditional acceptance of God's will and good spirit in order to purify and enhance the greater life of the small self. spirit is a flow to tap into.

A spiritual person has surrendered the small self into acceptance of God's will and unconditional devotion to the transcendent mystery of God's framework. Attention rests without expectation on the formless and nameless in recognition of the manifest divinity throughout. Spirit is a flow to express." [26]

CONSONANTS WITH 'A'

THE LETTERS 'AD'

You have a desire to be perfect in God's eyes. You work for God and no one else. Your soul wants you to understand that God isn't perfect and so you are not expected to be perfect either. Your goal is to do your best and allow God to do the rest, as you are hard on yourself.

THE LETTERS 'AL'

You have insecurities that you would not like anyone else to notice. These insecurities are based on having an untrue belief for one of

---

[26] Pete Ashly on Quora May 30, 2015 with his permission to print.

your core beliefs. To validate yourself you seek approval from others. Your soul wishes for you to sort out why you believe what you do so that you can eradicate that mistaken core belief. Your goal is to have faith in yourself without becoming self-centered, egotistical, or deceptive.

THE LETTERS 'AN'

You want to make the world a better place. In order to do so you have chosen to become persnickety, accented with acute observation skills as one who clearly sees the differences between actions and words. You can also be a bit nerdy, over religious or too scientific.

Your soul does not understand why you feel like you don't fit with everyone else . Your soul knows you are a seeker who uses sources outside of yourself to help you find yourself. You also expect spirituality to be practical, thus you expect spirituality to be able to be applied to life situations instantly.

Your goal is to use your spiritual knowledge to assist others and to minimize other people's discomforts. This brings you into contact with people who can further your spiritual growth.

In other words, do good, be good, and get rewarded with more spiritual understandings.

THE LETTERS 'AND'

You are highly passionate about one thing. Your soul is passionate about one thing. Your goal is to find that one thing that you love, for when you do you will blossom into an amazing individual.

THE LETTERS 'ANN'

You like to be prepared for whatever happens, and thus you store extras of everything, just in case you may need something later. Your soul has experienced tragedy and wants to protect you this time. Your goal is not to let previous tragic experiences determine your actions now, or cause you to fear in the present lifetime.

THE LETTERS 'AR'

You speak your mind and can be quite direct. This is because you have fairness issues that cause you to fight for others. Yet, your soul is not comfortable standing up for itself. Your soul wants you to learn how to stand up for yourself without demeaning the ones who insulted you. Your goal is to let your voice be heard, and to learn the difference between what is considered fair versus what is what is considered just.

THE LETTERS 'ARA'

You mature early and are quite intelligent which can cause you to burn brightly. However, it can also cause you to burn out early. Your soul wants you to use your maturity to develop early and lead others in a positive direction early in their lives. Share your spiritual understandings to motivate others to want to learn about spirituality so that they can be more like you. Your goal is to help others understand what you understand, and to be a role model for them.

THE LETTERS 'ARK'

You have an aptitude for making money which translates into being a good provider. Your soul wants you to focus on spiritual things, instead of financial worries, or being concerned about survival. Your goal is to keep your focus on spiritual matters. In order to do this, you need to make a living, but not get lost in the material world, or become greedy in the material world, since creating a good income is so easy for you.

THE LETTERS 'ART'

You want your fair share. You see what others have and you want it too. Your soul wants you to be aware of what others have, and yet not want to possess what they have. Your goal is to appreciate the diversity in people's ability to acquire material goods without coveting their belongings. This is easier to do when you focus on spiritual growth versus material accumulation.

THE LETTERS 'ATTI'

Your personality is prone to addictions. Your soul wants you to be able to discern what constitutes a positive addiction versus a negative one. Your goal is not to act on any temptations that could be considered negative, regardless of what that addiction may be. Most often the challenge is alcohol, but it could be an addiction to a person, or a substance.

THE LETTERS 'DAN'

You have a pleasant personality that disarms others, yet you also have trickster or shyster energy present. You can be the good guy who works on catching the crooks, or you can be the bad guy who has convinced self that you are a good guy. This happens when you masquerade as a helpful servant, but when backed into a corner will take whatever action is necessary to get what you want, or to protect your secrets. So, you are either the person that exposes renegade offenders, or you are the renegade offender.

Your soul asks that you get to know you so well that you are congruent with whatever side of the field you are playing. Congruency is of utmost importance for you. Your goal, once you are congruent, is to choose to use your skills to expose deceptive practices, not to participate in them.

THE LETTERS 'GA'

You are extremely knowledgeable in your own field. Using this knowledge makes it easy for you to convince others that their own perspective is the right one. You are an agent of change as your thoughts and discussions with others motivates others to look at things differently.

Your soul knows that you have the power of

influence. You feel comfortable in situations where others do not. Your goal is to use your power in a positive way so that you positively affect others.

THE LETTERS 'HA'

You strive to be faultless as you hate being the brunt of a cosmic joke. Your soul wants you to know that you are here to learn how to land on your feet when you perceive tragedy has struck. Your goal is to stay positive as you move through life and not get discouraged when things don't go your way.

THE LETTERS 'MAC'

These letters indicate a family bonding. You feel you belonging to a clan or a group as your family sticks together right or wrong. Your soul feels its important to feel a sense of belonging. Your goal is to still have your own boundaries so that your group does not dictate to you how to feel and act.

THE LETTERS 'MAL'

You can be obnoxious, jealous and/or arrogant. MAL means malfeasance. Your soul wants you to consider being nice, to be the good guy versus the person who presents self one way publicly and yet feels differently inside. Thus, your actions and thoughts are incongruent. Your goal is to learn how to play nicely with others.

THE LETTERS 'MAN'
Your actions may irritate others. It does not matter whether you irritate others intentionally or unintentionally. Your soul wants you to realize why you feel the need to annoy others, and to realize what is truly bothering you. Your goal is to learn to how to have peace within yourself so you can then emanate that peace outwardly.

THE LETTERS 'NAN'
You love to spend other people's money. Your soul wants you to learn how to use all resources wisely, including money. Your goal is to utilize other people's resources as you do your own; to be just as thrifty with their money as you are with yours.

THE LETTERS 'RA'

You are susceptible to having others take things from you that you don't wish to give to them. This could happen on the physical, emotional, mental or spiritual level. When on the physical level, it could be having others steal from you, or you being raped. If on the mental level it could be that someone else takes credit for your work. There are many ways you can have something taken from you that you don't wish to give to another.

Your soul wants you to know what it feels like to share willingly and unwillingly. This is to balance previous thoughts and misunderstandings. it is important for you to see your reactions to injustice while simultaneously understanding and having compassion for the culprit's actions. Your goal is to focus on your own safety, always putting safety first and foremost while doing your best to see situations from everyone's perspective.

THE LETTERS 'RAY'

You are here to learn about entitlement issues, and to use your creative abilities to manifest for the good of the whole. Your soul wants you to appreciate what you have, and to appreciate what that you are able to manifest things for yourself; that you are not dependent on others. Your goal is to row your own canoe, and not to covet what others have, or depend on others for your sustenance.

CONSONANTS WITH THE 'E'

THE LETTERS 'ECE'

It would be best for you to be in charge only when your emotions are strong, as you struggle to be in charge when your emotions are out of balance. Said another way, you make great decisions when your emotions are stable and questionable decisions when emotionally disturbed.

Your soul wants you to realize the influence your emotions have on you and how you can attempt to bury or ignore your feelings. Your goal is to allow your emotions to flourish and yet not let them dominate your decisions.

THE LETTERS 'EDE'

You have an amazing ability to receive insights by using your intuition. You also have a tendency to gather clutter around you. The amount of clutter that is needed is directly proportional to your emotional stability. Your soul asks you to realize that clutter assists you in getting your thinking started. Without clutter, when everything is too neat around you, it is harder for you to think outside of the box. Your goal is to minimize your clutter, not eliminate it completely.

THE LETTERS 'EL'

You can be self serving as your self-confidence can run amok. This is due to your strong ego which causes you to feel you are above the rules. Others may say that you consider yourself invincible and irresistible.

Your soul wants you to reign in your ego as you are not impervious. Your soul appreciates your belief in self, and would like it if you used some of that bravado to also believe in a power higher than yourself. That does not mean simply acknowledging God, but to actually modify your behavior to match your understandings of God's ways. Your goal is to seek God, without thinking you are God.

THE LETTERS 'ELE'

Your emotions influence your self-confidence. As such, your self-assurance is inconsistent. Your soul wants you to know that regardless of how you are currently feeling, you have value. Your goal is to see your own value consistently.

THE LETTERS 'EN'

You are energetic, and even keeled emotionally. Your soul wants you to stay balanced regardless of the surprises that life can throw your way. Your goal is to stay flexible and stable.

THE LETTERS 'ENCE'

You have a fabulous ability to stay in control of yourself regardless of where your emotions currently are. Your soul wants you to show others how you use your coping skills in a myriad of circumstances. Your goal is to stay in control of your feelings, while not becoming callous.

THE LETTERS 'ENE'

You occasionally remember things incorrectly as your memory is affected by your emotions. Your organizational skills are affected by your emotions also. Your soul asks you to stabilize your emotions so that you can be productive regardless of how you are currently feeling. Your goal is to stay organized, and exercise that wonderful memory of yours, along with doing your best to see things how they really are, independent of how your emotions may want it to be.

THE LETTERS 'ENR'

You have a philanthropic nature and have a healthy appreciation of fine art. Your soul has blessed you with an ability to see what others cannot. Your goal is to use your talents and generosity in such a way that it benefits many.

THE LETTERS 'ER'

This combination is somewhat touchy, as it indicates attention to and preoccupation with sex. This can show up as sexual unease, or mixing emotions with truth in the area of sexuality, or having issues or neurosis around sex, infatuation with sex; or an insatiable sexual appetite.

Your soul wants you to balance your understanding of sexual energy with your desires so that you enjoy your physicality, yet you don't let it become your only desire. Your goal is to explore your sexual nature while remaining sensitive to other's desires which may or may not match your own. In other words, don't force your beliefs on others or cause them harm with your actions.

Remember that sexual energy and spiritual energy is the same energy, just directed differently. Perhaps, at times, redirecting your sexual energy can be of assistance.

THE LETTERS 'ERE'

You have a hard time seeing the truth when your emotions are unbalanced. When unstable you can be overly rebellious, plus your perceptions can become distorted. You are a person who enjoys taking action. So, you become capable of committing heinous, despicable acts when your perceptions are off due to your rebellious nature.

Your soul wants you to realize that your

judgment is not impartial and to use your wonderful mind in analyzing what really occurred versus what your emotions indicate occurred. Your goal is to think a long time before deciding to act on your thoughts when emotions are out of alignment.

THE LETTERS 'ESS'

There is one warning that your soul wishes for you to be aware… that is not to become a gossip. Your soul has plenty of reasons and excuses to justify your inclination to make things up to gain attention or to spread what you have heard.

Yes, you'll find out information about other people, but please use your knowledge wisely and not to gossip or hurt someone else. Your goal is to learn how to keep secrets, and not share all that you know.

THE LETTERS 'EVE'

You are charismatic when your emotions are stable. Your soul wishes for you to keep your emotions stable, or at the very least, not to act on your emotions when they are out of balance. Your goal is to use your charm in positive ways and not to take advantage of others when they find you charming.

THE LETTERS 'EXE'

You can be negativity personified. You can become fixed on a specific desired outcome, yet you may perceived things incorrectly and thus create errors where there are none. Your soul wants you to think before you overreact. Your goal is to look for the silver lining in all experiences so that you learn how to make lemonade out of lemons.

CONSONANTS WITH THE 'I'

THE LETTERS 'CIN'

You have a tendency to become impatient with others who do not yield to your assumed authority. Others may consider you a bit bossy. Your soul wants you to realize that you are no better, and no worse, than anyone else. When you assume control over someone else you are also assuming you know best. It is a hidden attempt to usurp someone else's power.

Your soul wants you to realize that you only need to be in charge when you are afraid that you are not as good as you think you are.

Your goal is not to go into fear as that is what initiates this controlling behavior. When you grasp the truth about control, and why people crave control, you will realize that you were only meant to be in charge of you, and no one else.

THE LETTERS 'HIM'

You have a predisposition to bond with others as you keep your covenants with them. Your soul wants you to monitor your thoughts so that they can be just as pure as your actions. Your goal is to be as congruent as possible in your thoughts and deeds.

THE LETTERS 'ICE'

You can start by being nice, but end up being icy or vice-versa. You want to do it all. Your soul wants you to monitor when you become icy, remembering that everyone is equally as important as yourself. So, don't hold back any of your love. Your goal is to act with compassion, but only when you feel it. Otherwise, stay neutral such that you don't come across as cold.

THE LETTERS 'IN'

You need to be in the know, or at least feel

that you know everything that is happening with the people around you. Your soul wants you to stay connected to others. Your goal is to be interested in others welfare because you care, versus not just wanting to know what is happening to the people around you as a protective measure for yourself, or so that you won't ever be surprised.

THE LETTERS 'LI'

You can be ever so clever when you want to be. Your soul wants you to find clever ways that work for you as long as you are still considerate of others. Your goal is to make sure you don't resort to any type of deceit to get your way, instead you rely on being ethically astute.

THE LETTERS 'SKI'

You have a wacky sense of humor that is delightful as long as you don't use it to put others down or belittle them in order to feel good about yourself. Your soul wants you to remain willing to be different and inventive. Your goal is to master what your soul wants for you, using your humor, without diverting into the negative ways humor can be used.

THE LETTERS 'TRI'

Your have a challenge regarding money. This can show up in deceitful ways or by over spending what you do have. Your soul wants you to become wise in how you use your resources. Your goal is become incredibly honest in regards to money, and finances in general, while never taking advantage of other people and their finances.

CONSONANTS WITH THE 'O'

THE LETTERS 'GOR'

You have a tendency to self-sabotage which is an attitude that is getting in your way of success. This causes you to have a tough, difficult road, with numerous setbacks before you finally get to achieve. Your soul wants you to put aside your personal fears that cause you to sabotage your own dreams. Your goal is to achieve your dreams without causing unnecessary setbacks.

THE LETTERS 'JO'

You do not tolerate authoritarianism

anywhere or from anyone as you don't want to be told what to do. You can create whatever you desire once you make up you mind to do so. You are productive; a good person who is competent and good to others.

Your soul wants you to be powerful and to learn how to follow your own lead. You can listen to others, but your soul wants you to make your own decisions, relying only on what you feel is right. Your goal is to be you, all of you, without showing any domineering behavior towards others. To copy the military slogan, you are to be all that you can be.

THE LETTERS 'OB'

You are narcissistic and will do whatever is necessary to gain authority over others as you have an insatiable appetite for power. Your soul wants you to use your drive to benefit others, and not to take advantage of them. Your goal is to focus on more people than just you and yours.

THE LETTERS 'ON'

You are a skeptic by nature, have an aptitude for logic, which is can be used in either math, music or mechanics. Your focus must be on spiritual growth and awareness and then the living your knowledge, for you have nothing to offer the world if you remain in the same old universal belief system. If you are clearing old energies and resolving old karmic situations, allow the process, but do not get so enmeshed in them that you spend the rest of your life laying on a couch declaring that you can do nothing because you are clearing.

Your soul says follow your instincts. If you are guided toward some action, do it. If you are guided to be silent and hold the energy of Light for some world situation or person, do it. It is a time in which old solutions and rules no longer work so it is fruitless to keep trying to make them work.

THE LETTERS 'OR'

You speak your mind and can be quite direct. This is because you have fairness issues which causes you to fight for others and you are able to stand up for yourself. Your soul wants you to continue to stand up for yourself and others without demeaning the ones who have insulted you. Your goal is to use your voice for justice.

THE LETTERS 'ORG'

Self-deception is the will to deceive the self; the will not to believe in yourself. You are a king in the area of self-deception and self-sabotage. Your soul wants you to support yourself without getting in your own way. Your goal is to reel in your ego so that you can succeed.

THE LETTERS 'RO'

This is a karmic letter combination as 'RA' and 'RO' indicates people will attempt to take from you that which is not theirs but rightfully belongs to you. This can mean rape, or theft, being the victim of a crime, or having your ideas stolen. This occurs so that you can see, feel, and hopefully understand what crime feels like from a victim's point of view.

Your soul wants you to come from a place of compassion and understanding, as well as being able to recover from a violation without wanting revenge or falling into a victim mentality. This will undo the karma that you previously incurred.

Your goal is to heal from the experience and not want revenge. That implies true healing, so that your future is not interrupted, or changed, due to troublesome experiences. Lastly, your goal is to find compassion in your heart for your perpetrator. Not to forget what happened, but to be able to forgive the perpetrator so that you can balance your previous karma, and to assist you in not mistakenly wanting revenge.

CONSONANTS WITH THE 'U'

THE LETTERS 'BRU'

You can be a hypocrite, manipulating situations by saying one thing and meaning another in order to control the ones around you. You can be paranoid, assuming others are out to get you. This can cause you to have acute hostility towards others. Your soul wants you to use your charm to connect with others versus feeling ostracized from others. Your goal is to bond with others without needing to make them fellow warriors who are fighting on your behalf.

THE LETTERS 'JU'

You are an over achiever in at least one area of your life, because you combine your intelligence, your high self-esteem, and your ability to work hard with your practical nature and sense of humor. Your soul wishes for you to use these skills to support others as well as yourself. Your goal is to do so without losing your sense of self.

THE LETTERS 'LUC'

You have intermittent bouts of low self-esteem because you forget how to love yourself. Thus you struggle to maintain balance between being fully involved with multitudes of people and needing periods of respite.

Your soul wants you to balance your generous nature with your own needs so that you don't require those long interludes of aloneness. Your goal is to love you and treat you as well as you treat others.

THE LETTERS 'RU'

You appear appreciative, but often are not. You can feel unjustly accused, even as you present differently in public than who you really are privately. Your soul knows who you really are and totally accepts you. Your goal is to accept all of who you are, even the noncongruent parts of you. Be careful not to take advantage of others while you are figuring out exactly who you are.

THE LETTERS 'QU'

You are naturally comfortable in the limelight and easily attract others to you. Your soul is stable and wants you to take others adoration without letting it go to your head. Your goal is to stay gregarious and to enjoy the limelight as you deserve to be there.

THE LETTERS 'SUS'

You have an adventurous spirit with no apparent fears. You definitely don't want to miss out on anything and thus push yourself into unfamiliar territory. Your soul wants you to feel comfortable in multiple settings. Your goal is experience as many aspects of life as possible and to be comfortable with whatever life brings to you, regardless if you deem it positive or negative.

THE LETTERS 'UP'

You invite people to use you, to take advantage of you. Your soul asks that you balance what you need with what others want from you. Your goal is mix with others without resenting them for wanting so much from you. Having strong boundaries will help you in this endeavor.

THE LETTERS 'UR'

You have intermingled fantasy with reality to such an extent that you can become a psychological liar, being so convincing in your lies that you even fool yourself. Your soul sees your incredible charm, and seriousness in living the life of your dreams. It also knows you are tempted to become harsh and judge others or to seek revenge for perceived injustices that were done to you. Your soul recognizes that you have a challenge with discernment.

Your goal is to see things clearly for what they are and not how you want them to be. Your goal is to develop your discernment so that it can be a useful tool. Do not let your desire to see life through rose colored glasses cloud reality around you.

CONSONANTS WITH THE 'Y'

THE LETTERS 'CY'

You are a natural hero as you need to rescue others while staying in control of a situation. You are a natural super hero as you are so good to others. Your soul recognizes your ability to be wonderful to others and wishes for you to also be good to yourself. Your goal is to remember to make time for you as you tend to give so much to others that there is not enough time for yourself.

THE LETTERS 'LY'

You self-sacrifice in an attempt to keep others happy. You are a rescuer who successfully flies by seat of your pants. Your soul appreciates your desire to be of assistance to others, and yet wants you not to rescue others when the other person truly does not need rescuing. Your goal is to learn when to be of assistance, and when to stand back and simply assist by believing in the other's ability to rescue self.

THE LETTERS 'LYN'

You are busy releasing egoist issues from the

past so that you may be of maximum service to others. Your soul wants you to continue to pursue your spiritual interests while also serving others. Your goal is to keep your ego in balance, as you can easily be insulted, and then turn away from your pursuits.

THE LETTERS 'YN'

You are willing to self-sacrifice when necessary for the good of the community since you are so service oriented. You are a natural philosopher. Your soul knows that it can present itself as a bit conceited and rather obnoxious. Your goal is to keep your ego in check so that you don't feel the need to go negative with belligerent behavior.

THE LETTERS 'YT'

You prefer staying in the adolescent phase of life as your little child inside loves to play. Your soul wants you to grow up while simultaneously nurturing your inner child. Your goal is to blossom where you are planted keeping your inner child present in as many moments as appropriate.

THE LETTERS 'YV'

You are a natural leader who is willing to work just as hard as you ask others to work because you want people who work for you to continue to grow. Your soul understands that you will become the center of controversy since you believe that the ends justify the means. Your goal is to keep your ethics high while accomplishing all that you will do.

CHAPTER 9:
MIDDLE AND LAST NAMES

"All ancient names pointed out a person's true nature." The Philosophy of Astrology p, 46

Our first name reveals the essence of who we are. Middle names indicate where we go when we are under stress. We go to qualities and characteristics of the middle name as those are the attributes that we are most familiar. The reason for this is because those are the qualities that we have perfected over the last life for those of you who have embraced the concept of reincarnation. The last name indicates one's environmental influences.

A friend of mine was reading Theresa Caputo's

book, There is More to Life Than This, and couldn't wait to share a story in the book that confirms my previous statement that our middle names indicate the previous life lived. The story was about Melanie, who came to see the Long Island Medium, five months after her husband, Leon, died. Theresa also stated that the soul of the dead husband was returning and would occupy the new baby's body. Melanie's dead husband informed Theresa, "If she doesn't sense or see Leon anymore, this means that his soul was reborn in her child." Theresa informs Melanie and states, "Either way, the minute you hold him, you will feel that something is different about this baby,' I said. She told me that she plans to give the child the middle name of Leon." [27]

Our last name indicates our environment. We learn from our environment because of an extreme; either the quality was present and easy to copy or the quality was so missing that it became obvious that the quality is necessary. In the first case, individuals imitate their

---

[27] There is More to Life Than This by Theresa Caputo with Kristina Grish, published by Atria, a division of Simon and Schuster, Inc., 2013, p. 212-213

environment. In the second case, individuals find out for themselves how to incorporate that quality into their life. Either way, the environment influences us to incorporate a particular quality into our life.

When you are reading the interpretation of the letters in the middle name, know that these are intermittent characteristics. These qualities will be worked on occasionally, but will not be your focus for this lifetime as you previously had an entire lifetime to work on these qualities. Thus, you are simply fine tuning them this time around.

The environmental influences are here to help you accomplish those qualities that are in your first name. They assist you in seeing things from different angles than you would have initially seen something. What is most important is that you conquer the challenges in your first name. It is best that we work on those attributes first and foremost.

When we use a name other than our birth name we are stating that we are focusing on other attributes that may, or may not, be similar to the ones we initially wished to master.

Our soul, prior to coming into the current life, had help in creating goals and learning experiences that would help the soul to grow. These are represented in the original birth name.

We are here to learn the qualities that are represented in our birth names. Once learned, it is easy to change our name, thereby giving ourselves new goals. New names equal new personalities. However, the birth name, our original contract with God for this lifetime, does not change.

Made in the USA
Las Vegas, NV
11 April 2021